# COUNTRY OF THE THAMES

THE ABBEY CHURCH OF DORCHESTER

*Frontispiece*

# COUNTRY OF THE THAMES

By

ANNAN DICKSON

" *The river glideth at his*
*own sweet will* "

LONDON

CHATERSON LTD

5 JOHNSON'S COURT, FLEET STREET, E.C.4

*This is a* CROSS-COUNTRY BOOK. *The following titles have already been published in this series:* CHILTERN FOOTPATHS *by Annan Dickson and* FOOTPATHS OF THE KENT-SUSSEX BORDER *by Joseph Braddock.*

BOOK
PRODUCTION
WAR ECONOMY
STANDARD

THIS BOOK IS PRODUCED IN COMPLETE CONFORMITY WITH THE AUTHORIZED ECONOMY STANDARDS

*First published 1948*

PRINTED IN GREAT BRITAIN BY RICHARD CLAY AND COMPANY, LTD.
BUNGAY, SUFFOLK.

# CONTENTS

# LIST OF ILLUSTRATIONS

vi

# ROUTES AND DISTANCES

## CHAPTER ONE

### *Main Road Runs*

| | | | |
|---|---|---:|---|
| From London to Windsor | . . . . . . . | 23 | miles |
| thence by Reading | . . . . . . . | 20 | ,, |
| Wantage | . . . . . . . | 25 | ,, |
| Faringdon | . . . . . . . | 9 | ,, |
| Cricklade | . . . . . . . | 14 | ,, |
| to Cirencester | . . . . . . . | 7 | ,, |

98

| | | | |
|---|---|---:|---|
| From Cirencester by Fairford | . . . . . . . | 9 | miles |
| Lechlade | . . . . . . . | 4 | ,, |
| Witney | . . . . . . . | 12 | ,, |
| Oxford | . . . . . . . | 12 | ,, |
| Dorchester | . . . . . . . | 9 | ,, |
| Henley | . . . . . . . | 14 | ,, |
| to London | . . . . . . . | 37 | ,, |

97

### *Intermediate Round Tours*

| | | |
|---|---:|---|
| London to Oxford direct, via Maidenhead . . . . | 60 | miles |
| via Beaconsfield . . . . | 57 | ,, |

| | | |
|---|---:|---|
| Oxford to Abingdon . . . . . . . . | 6 | miles |
| ,, ,, Woodstock . . . . . . . | 8 | ,, |
| ,, ,, Witney . . . . . . . | 12 | ,, |

| | | |
|---|---:|---|
| London to Reading direct . . . . . . | 40 | miles |

| | | |
|---|---:|---|
| Reading to Streatley . . . . . . . | 10 | miles |
| thence by Wallingford . . . . . . . | 7 | ,, |
| and Shillingford . . . . . . . | 2 | ,, |
| to Goring . . . . . . . | 9 | ,, |
| return via Mapledurham . . . . . . | 6 | ,, |
| to Reading . . . . . . . | 5 | ,, |

39

## CHAPTER TWO

### *Paths and By-roads*

From Wallingford (G.W.R. branch from Cholsey and Moulsford)—walk or bus to Brightwell (3 miles), walk to Wittenham Clumps (1 mile), down to Day's Lock (1 mile), to Dorchester (1 mile), *thence* bus to Oxford; *alternatively*, from Little Wittenham (1 mile), road to Long Wittenham (1 mile), Clifton Hampden (2 miles) and Burcot (1 mile), *thence* to Oxford Road (1 mile) for bus to Oxford (9 miles) or bus to Littlemore Station (G.W.R.) (4 miles); *or*, from Long Wittenham, road to Appleford (3 miles), Sutton Courtenay (2 miles) and Culham (1 mile), to Abingdon (2 miles) (G.W.R. or bus to Oxford).

## CHAPTER THREE

### *Country Lanes*

From Aylesbury (43 miles from London) to Quainton (6 miles) and Whitchurch (5 miles), *thence* by Cublington (3 miles) and Aston Abbots (2 miles) to Weedon (3 miles) and back to Aylesbury (3 miles) (a 22-mile round); *or*, Quainton to Waddesdon (3 miles), by Over and Nether Winchendon and Chearsley to Long Crendon (8 miles), via Thame (2 miles) to Cuddington (4 miles) and Haddenham (2 miles), from Haddenham to Kingsey by lane or field-path (1 mile), via Towersey (2 miles) to Thame (2 miles) (29–30 miles from Aylesbury); *or*, Haddenham, via Aston Sandford to Ilmer (3 miles) and across fields to Towersey (2 miles) for Thame (2 miles) (G.W.R. to Oxford 14 miles, or London 44 miles).

## CHAPTER FOUR

### *By-ways Among Oxfordshire Villages*

From Thame (14 miles on London side of Oxford) by Moreton (1 mile through fields or 2 miles by road) to Tetsworth (2 miles), by Stoke Talmage and Clare Hill to Cut Mill (4 miles) (8–9 miles from Thame); *thence*, from Cut Mill by Cuxham (1 mile) and Brightwell Baldwin (1 mile) to Ewelme (2 miles), thence by Crowmarsh and North Stoke to Goring (8 miles) for G.W.R. main line (21 miles from Thame); *or*, from Cut Mill, right for Chalgrove (2 miles), Berrick Salome (2 miles) and Benson (2 miles), *thence* to Wallingford (3 miles) for G.W.R. branch line (18 miles from Thame).

## CHAPTER FIVE

### *Roads around Oxford*

From Quainton (6 miles beyond Aylesbury from London) to Grendon Under-wood (5 miles), Ludgershall (4 miles), by Piddington and Arncot to Ambrosden

(5 miles), to Charlton-on-Otmoor (6 miles) and Islip (2 miles), to Beckley (3 miles), on to Studley (2 miles) and Boarstall (2 miles), up to Brill (2 miles), down to Long Crendon (4 miles)—a 41-mile round from Aylesbury; and Oxford, via Shabbington, Waterperry, and Wheatley, is 13 miles westward: Thame, 2 miles south-west.

From Oxford (Magdalen Bridge) Iffley lies 2 miles southward, Sandford Lock is 2 miles farther, and Abingdon 4 miles farther still. For Cumnor, most direct way—road from Carfax (4 miles), *thence* to Bablock-hithe (3 miles), Stanton Harcourt (2 miles) and Eynsham (3 miles). Eynsham to Oxford, 6 miles.

# CHAPTER SIX

## *By-roads in the Hills*

From Bicester (17 miles west of Aylesbury and 60 miles from London) by Souldern (7 miles) to Aynho (2 miles) and Farthinghoe (5 miles) to Middleton Cheney (2 miles)—16 miles from Bicester.

From Middleton Cheney by " Banbury Lane " to Banbury (4 miles), by Bloxham (4 miles) and Swerford (4 miles) to Chipping Norton (6 miles), *thence* by Charlbury (Evenlode Valley) to Woodstock and Oxford (20 miles), making 38 miles from Middleton Cheney and 54 miles from Bicester to Oxford;

*or*, on from Middleton Cheney to Thorpe-Mandeville (4 miles), to Culworth (2 miles), and Chipping Warden (4 miles), making 26 miles from Bicester. From Chipping Warden, left for Wardington and right at Williamscot (3 miles) for Cropredy, Mollington, and Warmington (6 miles) to Edge Hill (2 miles), *thence* by Sibford Ferris (9 miles) and Hook Norton (3 miles) to Chipping Norton (5 miles)—54 miles from Bicester; to Oxford (20 miles), making 74 miles from Bicester;

*or*, from Chipping Warden by the " Welsh Road " to Lower Boddington (4 miles) and Wormleighton (3 miles), by Fenny Compton (2 miles) and Avon Dasset (2 miles) to Edge Hill (3 miles). South to Great Rollwright (11 miles), by Adlestrop (6 miles), and Stow-on-the-Wold (3 miles) to Naunton, upper Windrush valley (6 miles). By Andoversford—head of Coln—(7 miles) and " St. Paul's Epistle ", down Chatcombe Pitch to Seven Springs (4 miles), down Churn valley by Colesbourne and North Cerney to Cirencester (12 miles), making from Bicester, 89 miles.

## *By-roads in the Levels*

From Cirencester, right (S.S.W.) for Thames Head (3 miles), by South Cerney to Cricklade (9 miles); *thence* Roman Road S.E., and left for Highworth (8 miles), by Faringdon (6 miles) to Stanford-in-the-Vale (4 miles), left at East Challow for Wantage (6 miles) left for Abingdon (G.W.R. branch) (10 miles), making, from Cirencester, 46 miles; *or*, from Cricklade, left for Fairford (8 miles), right for Lechlade (4 miles), to Kelmscott (3 miles), and by Clanfield (5 miles), Bampton (2 miles) and Witney (6 miles) to Oxford (12 miles), making, from Cirencester, 52 miles.

## CHAPTER SEVEN

### *Hill and Valley By-roads*

From Theale Station, G.W.R., to Sulhampstead Abbots (2 miles), Silchester (4 miles), Highclere (10 miles) and Newbury (8 miles), making 24 miles.

From Aldermaston Station, G.W.R., to Beenham (2 miles), Bucklebury Common (5 miles), Bucklebury Village (2 miles), Stanford Dingley (2 miles), Bradfield (2 miles)—13 miles from Aldermaston to Bradfield—*thence* to Pangbourne, G.W.R. (6 miles), making 19 miles; *or*, Bradfield to Ashampstead (4 miles) and Aldworth (2 miles) for Streatley, G.W.R. (3 miles), making, from Aldermaston, 22 miles.

### *Over the Berkshire Downs*

From Newbury (G.W.R., or road, 57 miles from London) to Lambourn (12 miles), thence N.W. by downland track to Waylands Smithy (5 miles), to White Horse Hill and Uffington Castle (1 mile), East to Segsbury Camp (road down to Wantage, 2 miles) (6 miles), from Segsbury by the Ridge Way to Blewbury Downs (Churn Station) (9 miles), *thence* by Fair Mile (or, if still a bombing-ground, by Unhill Bottom) to Moulsford (4 miles), for Cholsey and Moulsford Station, G.W.R. main line (1 mile), making 26 miles from Lambourn (25 miles of open down).

## CHAPTER EIGHT

### *Paths and By-ways*

From Reading, through Sonning and Twyford, to Knowle Hill (London Road) (9 miles), left for Warren Row and Cockpole Green, to Remenham Hill (4 miles), by Hurley (4 miles), Temple (3 miles), Bisham (1 mile), to Marlow (1 mile), making, from Reading to Marlow, avoiding main roads, 22 miles.

From Marlow, by-roads to Burroughs Grove (2 miles), footpath to Little Marlow (2 miles), and to Spade Oak Ferry (1 mile), in all, 5 miles; *or*, from Burroughs Grove, footpaths by Lower Winchbottom to Sheepridge (4 miles) and 1 mile to Spade Oak, making 7 miles; *or*, road from Burroughs Grove to Handy Cross (2 miles), to Flackwell Heath (3 miles), to Well End (2 miles), and to Spade Oak Ferry (1 mile), making 10 miles.

From Spade Oak Ferry to Winter Hill (1 mile), to Bourne End Ferry (1 mile), to Hedsor Church (1 mile), *thence* to Cookham (1 mile) and Maidenhead (3 miles), making 7 miles.

## CHAPTER NINE

### Lanes and By-roads

Bourne End (G.W.R.) or Well End, to Cores End (1–2 miles); *thence* lane to Wooburn Common (2 miles), and paths to Beaconsfield (3 miles), making 7 miles; *or*, Cores End to Hedsor (1 mile), to Dropmore (1 mile), Littleworth Common (1 mile), by Burnham Beeches (1 mile) to Burnham Gores (2 miles), to Burnham Station, G.W.R. (1 mile), making 7 miles; *or*, by path from Burnham Beeches to Dropmore (1 mile), by-road to Cliveden (3 miles), to Hedsor Hill (1 mile), making 9 miles from Cores End (1 mile from Bourne End Station, G.W.R., or bus to Maidenhead or High Wycombe).

## CHAPTER TEN

### Hill and River By-paths

Footpath from Hedsor Hill to Cores End (1 mile), paths to Flackwell Heath (2 miles), by Glory Mill to Wooburn Green (2 miles), up to Berghers Hill (1 mile), to Hedsor Wharf (2 miles), Cookham Bridge across fields (1 mile), Cookham Dean to Winter Hill (2 miles), to Quarry Woods (2 miles), path to suburbs of Maidenhead (3 miles) for G.W.R., 28 miles to London. 16 miles of paths.

### Maps

Bartholomews' half-inch, " Surrey ", " Berks and Wilts ", and " Oxfordshire ".

Ordnance Survey one inch to mile, " Oxford and Henley-on-Thames ", and adjoining sheets.

THE WHITE HORSE OF UFFINGTON

## CHAPTER ONE

## A VERY GENERAL SURVEY

THE Thames is essentially a river of the country. Although the majority of the people to whom it is " The River " happen to be townsfolk, it is " The River " to them because it forms their readiest means of escape from their workaday towns.

Over a dozen major and minor streams contribute to make the River Thames what it is, and the term " Thames Valley " has a delightful elasticity. There are bodies with " Thames Valley " forming part of their titles whose activities centre upon Richmond and Kingston. There is a Thames Valley Traction Company, whose bus services cover most of the roads between Windsor and Oxford, and between Aylesbury and Newbury. The Thames Valley Branch of the Council for the Preservation of Rural England casts a sharp though benevolent eye over the main stream from Cricklade to Staines; and the Thames Conservancy keeps many pairs of eyes, quite as sharp and no less benevolent, alert and observant over the whole catchment area.

Take the Thames Valley, then, as lying inside the North Downs, the Berkshire Downs, and the Cotswold—a great oval covering hundreds of square miles of river-valley, upland and hill, to be enjoyed alike by motorist, cyclist, and pedestrian. Probably a combination of all three modes of travel, in the order given, would most quickly turn acquaintance into fast friendship.

A good day's run in a car, by Windsor, Reading, Want-

age, Faringdon, and Cricklade, might reach Cirencester by early afternoon. A return through Fairford, Witney, Oxford, Dorchester, and Henley, would bring the mileage well over two hundred. Too much for a day? Certainly, if seeing either the towns or the country is expected; but that could come later.

It would come later if half the possible stops and detours were noted, for the variety of scene alone, apart from the history and interest of every one of those towns, might induce mental indigestion; yet this is one way to gain a general idea of the possibilities in prospect to suit any individual taste.

The next step might be a quick run out and home, with a leisurely potter around Abingdon or Woodstock; or it might be a riverside round of Streatley, Wallingford, Shillingford, Goring, and Mapledurham. The pottering will increase, and the mileage drop unmourned, as those towns, and the villages and the plain, simple country in between, begin to get their grip.

There are ardent, hearty cyclists who pedal hard out and home and all the time, for whom mileage is a more persistent god. Others, more discriminating, entrust self and cycle to the Great Western Railway, leave one express at King-ham, and board another at Didcot, having pottered to some purpose through Shipton-under-Wychwood, Bamp-ton, and Charney Bassett. For them also, unfamiliar ground can thus be reached at many points, and within distance of many more such alluring place-names.

And walking—the only way of really getting to know the country? It would be a mistake to hold up the Thames Valley as walking country pure and simple. The distances, out and back and intermediate, call for some more rapid form of transport if one is to cover a tithe of the ground, and for that purpose the G.W.R., and the bus services of the Thames Valley and of the City of Oxford, will be welcome. Another reason is that the scenery is not con-centrated. Broad stretches of farmland, where both main

MAPLEDURHAM LOCK AND THE HILLS BEYOND.

THE RIVER BELOW WINDSOR CASTLE.

and minor roads run level near and far, cannot provide the sudden vistas of beauty that one enjoys among the hills.

This does not mean, however, that there are no views and no walking districts in the levels. There is an unforgettable point on the Roman road from Cirencester to Cricklade, where the great white horse of the White Horse Vale first shows on the Berkshire Downs. There is the moment of topping Sinodun Hill and sighting Whiteleaf Cross, twenty miles away in Buckinghamshire. There is the rounding of the bend of the prosaic main road by Clifton Hampden that brings one face to face with the venerable " Barley Mow " and the church on its height above the river. Also, for the walker, and for the walker only, there is the stretch of towpath from Cookham to Spade Oak Ferry, where he crosses not into Bucks, as he might think, but remains in Berkshire—for a strip of the northern bank is still Berks—and has the privilege of looking across the river again at Berkshire's own superlative Quarry Woods below Marlow. A tour of the towpath, in fact, is one good way of seeing both river and country from a fresh angle.

Those who care to follow up these suggestions by exploring for themselves will find ample scope, for in such a wide area not more than a fraction of its interest can be recorded; and lack of mention in this book does not mean lack of attraction. There are, indeed, few English towns and villages that have not some charm, and this is specially noticeable among the communities that have grown up, through so many centuries of living history, along and near the Thames.

Speaking generally, and without undue pandering to classification mania, the Thames divides into three distinct sections. Between London and Reading it has always been the Thames. From Reading to Wallingford it is, comparatively, a " New Cut ". Above Wallingford it is a gathering of many head-waters.

SHILLINGFORD BRIDGE JOINING BERKS AND OXFORDSHIRE.

LECHLADE CHURCH SPIRE BY THE WINDING UPPER THAMES.

These divisions of the river are based on geological developments of remarkable interest, which may be studied in such books as Lord Avebury's *Scenery of England* or Professor Dudley Stamp's *Britain's Structure and Scenery*. The Thames has always seemed so pre-eminently the great river of southern England that it may come as a surprise to hear of the small beginnings here implied; but this splitting-up will be justified as the survey progresses.

Up to forty miles westward from London, a colour-contoured map shows a green expanse, thirty miles wide, between Chilterns and North Downs, with only a few insignificant heights here and there. Those minor undulations, however, will provide some excellent view-points. Every valley-curve round those elevations—curves which make the river take some sixty-five miles to cover the thirty-mile straight line between Reading and

Teddington—means a corresponding vantage-point for seeing both river and surrounding country.

The Reading–Wallingford section is only ten miles long, but it contains the crux of the geological problem. The hills stand high and close, with 500-ft. heights only a couple of miles apart, where farms climb up, as far as cultivation can struggle, towards the beechwoods and fir copses above. Even though riverside bungalows suggest season-tickets and seem to spell " dormitory ", these excrescences soon shrink to their rightful proportions; for on either side one can quickly climb high enough to come to the astounding realization that this River Thames has actually worn its channel through the ridge that once reached continuously across its present bed.

Once above Goring, the whole scene and atmosphere combine to make one ready to accept whatever explanation geology can offer. It is a different river. The banks

EAST HENDRED, ONE OF MANY INTERESTING VILLAGES UNDER THE BERKSHIRE DOWNS.

CLIFTON HAMPDEN, ON THE RIVERSIDE ROUTE TO OXFORD.

broaden out into far-stretching meadows with ditches and runnels intersecting them everywhere.  Roads branch off through cornfields to Ipsden, to Aston Tirrold, to Britwell and the Brightwells (very different villages but all charming, whether it be the Brightwell of Berks, or Brightwell Baldwin or Brightwell Uppertown of Oxfordshire).  The river has a brisk yet unhurried flow; here, a long straight reach from Shillingford Bridge looks down to Benson church standing at the far bend backed by the Chiltern beechwoods; there, a series of twisting curves brings one suddenly, almost unnoticed although they have been waiting there all the time, close under the steep sharp hills of Sinodun, with the clumps of Wittenham poised so gracefully on their summits.

Here at Sinodun one comes at once upon the key point of the whole Upper Thames.  The hills command an astonishing sweep of country towards the higher hills where all the upper tributaries take their rise.  Up the main valley towards Oxford and beyond, up the Vale of White Horse, up towards the Vale of Aylesbury northwards, and up to the long dim line of Cotswold foothills, Wittenham Clumps survey it all.  Conversely there are few points of any eminence up-river, and few stretches of country road or river-bank for many miles around, from which one cannot catch a sight of that pair of tree-clumps, shapely and natural and perfectly placed, which appear so fittingly from whatever point they are seen.

## CHAPTER TWO

## THE KEY TO THE UPPER THAMES

No apology is offered for stressing the pre-eminence of Sinodun Hill as a view-point for the Upper Thames. It is even hoped that many who succumb to the attraction of Wittenham Clumps will enjoy a study of the neighbourhood, before going on to explore beyond.

Though high above the river, the Clumps are readily accessible from several sides, and a pilgrimage to the top is recommended, not for the view alone, but for the satisfying sense it gives one of being able to picture the Thames as a whole.

From here, as far as the limits of vision and beyond, the gathering together of the Thames can be realized. All the way from Thames Head beyond Cirencester the river has been picking up other streams from left and right, but keeping, in spite of infinite minor windings, a persistently eastward course, until it strikes the ring of hills round Oxford. It tries to circle their northern rim, but meets the Evenlode, its biggest confluent so far, and turns again eastward. There the Cherwell seems to take charge and makes the Thames keep it company southward, even westward round to Abingdon. There, the Ock is pouring eastward, and the river's tortuous, almost tortured, twistings, east and south again, seem explicable only by the theory of the continuous chalk ridge that formerly made Chilterns and Berkshire Downs one. Any slight depression in that ridge, above where Basildon and Whitchurch now stand, would be enough to make rain-water concentrate there and wear a deeper and deeper gully. Eventually this hollow wore back and down, clear through the ridge to the water-level beyond; and what had been a minor hill-stream joining the Kennet at Reading was swollen by the volume of water it had " captured "—volume sufficient to multiply many times the erosive power of the stream on its chalky banks.

Such is the bare outline of one era in the river's history. Its geography, up-stream and down again, can be mapped out, in what detail one chooses, from the vantage-point of Wittenham.

The Clumps can be approached by a variety of routes. A walker from Wallingford (assisted by bus to Brightwell for a look at the church and the many-angled streets) will find a field-path to the right, just where the road to Didcot turns away left over mile upon mile of not very inviting levels. The path chooses the better part, for, after tra-versing a couple of pasture-fields, it comes upon a great

ONE OF THE WITTENHAM CLUMPS, NEAR WALLINGFORD.

swelling rise and dip of plough or wheat or stubble according to the season. Choose stubble-time, if possible, when hares jump up close by and bound away out of sight. Continue over the shoulder of Brightwell Barrow, down and up again, and a sharper rise leads to the great earthwork defending the eastern Clump, and up that earthwork the tramper must find his own way.

Another excellent approach to the Clumps is by river. From Day's Lock, a couple of delightful footbridges lead to the foot of the long straggling village of Little Wittenham. Hardly even a street, this succession of brick-and-timber cottages can be followed round the shoulder of the hill; or, from opposite the church entrance, a path strikes left, along the side of a gently-rising field. Then it strikes the hill and slants boldly up: a steep rise, but one takes it in quick time, for the view, broadening out to left and right—and behind, too, if one pauses to look—gives promise of still better things from the top. Leftwards towards Goring, the Chilterns and the Berkshire Downs converge on the richly-wooded gully where the last curves of the river can be seen disappearing. Over the lower woodlands to the right, the long flat stretch past Abingdon is bounded by the hills round Oxford. Half right, over the clear-cut shoulder of the hill, the Vale of White Horse opens up mile after mile, until, over the dip between the two summits, one meets in full view the long, clear line of the Berkshire ridge-top, a 700-ft. height of bare, open down seven miles away to the south. That is the moment to spread out the map for such a study of landmarks as one rarely gains from an elevation of a mere 350 feet. From here, as from nowhere else, one can plan tour upon tour of many sub-sections of the upper valley, and so make Wittenham not only the objective of one journey, but the start of many more.

HILLSIDE WOODS
ABOVE THE RIVER
AT GORING.

POPLARS BY THE
RIVER NEAR
STREATLEY.

RIVER COUNTRY BETWEEN CHILTERNS AND BERKSHIRE DOWNS.

One could " enthuse " for many pages over Wittenham Clumps; their history, their position, and the view they command on all sides. " God gave all men all earth to love ", and no one would thrust his personal predilections on other country-lovers; but the Clumps do exercise a special fascination. They stand aloft, yet not aloof, above two of the most charming reaches of all the rural Thames—up from Shillingford to Day's Lock, and down past Benson to Wallingford—visible at a fresh angle round every bend of the stream and from road after road near and far. They catch the eye of the hill-topper who surmounts White Horse Hill or Fair Mile Down, Whiteleaf Cross or Huntercombe Hill, just as they appear to the lane-plodder by Easington or Appleford or Drayton St. Leonard, and at every sight of them there comes a lifting up of the heart.

What is it that makes this pair of tree-groups, on a comparatively insignificant hummock, unique?

It is worth while pondering on the attraction of this particular hillock. It is essentially both in the country and of the country. Farm buildings dot the roads that surround it; stubble-field or pasture covers nearly all its surface; and at ploughing-time the tractors slice their threefold furrows round the Clumps themselves. The bus route to Wallingford market skirts its south-eastward fringe; the cottages, church, and manor-house of Little Wittenham curl round the west and north; and within sight of all that continuity of rural life, those twin summits look over a ten, twenty, thirty-mile sweep of typical English country. Perhaps that is their secret—that they have always been there. The changes they have seen, in that apparently unchanging countryside, would make a history of England if they could tell their tale in full.

Early British earthwork on the one hump, Roman vallum close below; pagan Danes chasing Alfred westward to Athelney, Birinus founding his bishopric at Dorchester; William the Conqueror fording the Thames at

A QUIET STRETCH OF RIVER AT SHILLINGFORD.

HARVESTING NEAR LITTLE WITTENHAM.

Wallingford to encircle London, John Hampden clashing with Prince Rupert at Chalgrove; orphan boys training to be colonial farmers at Turner's Court, Benson Aerodrome sending the latest Lightning up on its trial flights: all this history that the Sinoduns have seen, we glean from other sources. They themselves yield few records to antiquary or historian, and for an explanation of their peculiar attractiveness the country-lover must take them as they are. A passer-by may take them so much for granted as never to climb their summits; there are hills in view that over-top them by several hundreds of feet; yet from all those heights the Sinoduns seem to form a focal point.

That being so, and topographically always having been so, one appreciates the long-standing significance of the hills. Even in speculative geological prehistory that tells of an inland sea between the Chiltern–Berkshire chalk and the Cotswold–Clifton limestone, the Sinoduns probably stood as islands above its waters. Then the Goring Gap became a *fait accompli*—not by violent earth-convulsion, but by the natural working of geologically recognized forces that radically re-fashioned southern England—and the Thames became a great river.

It was this expansion of the Thames area that turned the river from a local stream into a national one.   The term " Thames Valley ", fitting enough below Reading, became a misnomer, because half the river's course now meandered across the southern midland plain.   Still the Sinoduns stood sentinel at a point more vital than ever.   Those severely practical early Britons, with their unerring eye for a strategic height, inevitably seized on Sinodun for their camp above the Thames.

The name of the Atrebates has been passed down to us by the Romans as the title of the aboriginal inhabitants of Berkshire.   What they called themselves, we hardly know

THE VILLAGE CROSS AT LONG WITTENHAM.

—Cymri, probably, or " comrades ", as most other tribes did—but they knew and feared their distant kinsmen— distant in blood, but all too near in location—the Dobuni of the Cotswold, beyond the river; and a river such as the Thames, though a perfectly good and recognizable tribal boundary, was only a minor obstacle to raiding parties skilled in the management of coracles.

The Dobuni had more rivers on which to practise their amphibious wiles than had the Atrebates on the waterless Berkshire Downs.  Their sorties would call for an ever-watchful eye along the southern bank; and here in Sinodun the Atrebates found a vantage-point ready to their purpose. From Goring nearly up to Abingdon, no point of the river could escape the lookout on Sinodun.  Its rise from the river-level made it wellnigh impregnable from three sides, and on its fourth side, southward, the main bulwark of the Downs stood at easy distance for signal, for reinforcement, or for direction of counter-attack up or down river.  It formed the ideal outpost, of which the ancestors of all true Berkshire folk, experts as regards survival of the fittest, were quick to avail themselves.

Roman strategy never neglected a commanding height. From Dorchester across the river a Roman road ran north-ward through Alchester (near Bicester, to be noticed later) on to Towcester. Traces of another road southward lead towards Silchester (known to the Romans as Calleva of the Atrebates, where parts of the Roman wall still surround the site of a city whose excavated remains form a remarkable collection in Reading Museum).  Sinodun thus controlled the Thames-crossing of a strategic highway linking Win-chester and Southampton Water with the road system of the Midlands and the North.

So it continued to do after Roman times, when dark ages indeed settled upon Britain.  The Danes, landing in

THE CHURCH AT SUTTON COURTENAY.

successive hordes on the low estuaries of the eastern
counties, pushed each other farther and farther inland.
From the Wash, their natural line of penetration through the
lowlands led them irresistibly south-westward between
Chilterns and Cotswolds, with the ready-made track of the
Icknield Way bringing their advance inevitably to this
section of the Thames.   The river was the boundary, more
or less, between Mercia and Wessex, when the Saxon
kingdoms emerged;   and even to-day the Thames forms
county boundaries for most of its length, even though its
function has become that of a link rather than a divider.

The reaches of the Thames itself that are visible from the
hills are rich in beauty as well as in history and interests.
Though by no means unknown, they can never lose their
attractiveness, and it would be doing less than justice to
Thames country to desert the main stream yet awhile, to
explore the tributaries to the neglect of Dorchester and
Benson, Sutton Courtenay and Clifton Hampden, to say
nothing of Abingdon and Wallingford.

These last two ancient towns are both places where it is
a delight to roam round street after street and come upon
a charmingly-designed and situated dwelling-house, or
inn, or market-house.   At Abingdon, group after group of
most pleasing alms-houses can thus be discovered; here,
also, rather curiously, various benefactors chose to add
successive aisles to the noble church of Saint Helen.   At
Wallingford there is still traceable the fairly clear line of
the old town wall; a surprising number of churches stood
within that wall in mediæval times (one must not say
" early times ", for Wallingford's early times lie far back in
the mists of antiquity).

The history and architecture of Abingdon and Wallingford, however, have been admirably sketched by the
author of *Highways and By-ways in Berkshire*, for the

benefit of those wanting fuller information. They will join with him in deploring the misfortune Abingdon is alleged to have inflicted on itself, by destroying most of the town records when accommodation for them became overtaxed. Even so, Abingdon abounds in the stuff of history.

Another historical corner of this district lies directly over the Thames from Sinodun. A square mile of ground, with rivers on three sides, must always have been a sound defensive locality and place of refuge. Though Dorchester is now little more than a large village, it was a bishopric centuries ago, one of the earliest in the Midlands. Actually, it covered most of the Midlands, for its bounds extended as far north as Lincoln.

So one could go on exploring the by-ways of the past that are so plentiful hereabouts, while the by-ways of the countryside await the explorer too. Even the main road from Dorchester to Oxford, skirting the woods of Nuneham Courtenay, has its beauties. Still more has the Abingdon

THE LITTLE CHURCH OF CLIFTON HAMPDEN.

THE ABBEY GATEWAY, ONE OF THE MANY HISTORIC BUILDINGS IN
ABINGDON.

road, passing the old, well-kept cottages of Clifton Hampden, where the little church makes a fine picture high above
the river.   Or from Sinodun one can take the lane that
runs straight at Long Wittenham village, where a thatched
cottage with dormer windows looking right down the road
between massive elm-boles seems to block the way.   But
the road curls round, past the village cross, seeming to
look for the river that has lost itself among pollard willows.
It soon appears, though, over a little weir, where punts
show that the river is not neglected here; they tempt one
to forsake the road and explore the river itself round the
alluring curves up and down stream.   Or another by-road
leads on westward by straight, level stretches until it turns
into the broad, grass-bordered street of Sutton Courtenay,

which stretches away from the river for nearly a mile. Here the timbered cottages, some thatched and some with weathered tiles, stand back from the chestnuts that shade the street.    They lead on to the church, notable for its Norman tower, its window-ornamentation, and the fine porch, as well as for the tomb of the first Lord Oxford and Asquith. At Sutton Courtenay the river is almost too attractive to leave, for from the backwater by the mill up the idyllic reach to Abingdon the Thames really is in the country and makes it possible to see the best of both at once.

This is a digression up the main river however; there was a mention earlier of exploring some of the tributary-country visible from Sinodun.    That tract of land lying northward beyond the Thames is a good part on which to begin.

## CHAPTER THREE

## THE THAMES AND THE THAME

FROM Sinodun, a sample of the fresher, unhurried world above the Goring Gap lies ready to hand—across the river beyond the ancient settlement of Dorchester. There, the line of the Roman road leads straight away northwards, and the River Thame flows southwards, anything but straight, to join the Thames.

Though the river runs between them, the hill of Sinodun and the peninsula between Thames and Thame must clearly have had close dealings in both peace and war. The crossing at Day's Lock presents no difficulty beyond the modest toll; worth far more than that is the view—first along the shaded backwater and then down the main stream—of the Clumps, which from here seem to tower into the sky. On the Oxfordshire side, one steps straight into the country— just fields, with grassy paths wandering away from the over-hanging hedges towards the low green mounds of the Dyke Hills that formed a defensive barrier from river to river.

Dorchester, as one approaches it across another flat half-mile, forms a picture difficult to describe. Timber-and-brick cottages form outliers from the row of higher, more dignified roofs that line the street and screen the Abbey church. Its tower can be seen above them all, but it is not until one alley or another threads its way into the main road that the size and the imposing length of the church can be appreciated. With its eight great windows in the nave, lofty roof, and noble tower, Dorchester Abbey is a worthy survival from the days of great church-building.

The variety of ancient architecture along the curving street and the number of old inns give proof of Dorchester's long standing as a halt on the Oxford road for mail-coaches of the past as for Oxford–Reading buses of the present.

That road can be left to its own devices for the present, however, for just beyond the town's end, where the Oxford and Abingdon roads part company, another by-way doubles back to the right. Its signpost points to Drayton St. Leonard and to a number of other places too, for this is the beginning of a considerable digression into the country of one of the Thames's most considerable tributaries.

Barely a mile below Day's Lock, the Thame River finds its way into the River Thames. It joins the main river so unobtrusively, among its rushes and marshy river-meadows, that coming upstream one can easily pass it unnoticed. Yet it is notable, both for the length of its meanderings— from the remote hill-pastures of North Buckinghamshire and the borders of Hertfordshire—and for the wide area of country that it drains—nearly the whole of the Vale of Aylesbury. More than that, the little River Thame likes to think that it joins with the better-known Isis to give the great Thames its classical name of Tamesis. South Oxfordshire folk stoutly maintain that the Thames is only the Thames below Dorchester, where Oxford's river, on receiving this worthy tribute, ceases to be the Isis.

This Thame river is one of the least known of all the Thames's tributaries, perhaps because it is such a thoroughly " country " stream. Even its name-town, of which more anon, stretches its broad High Street a mile away from the river that curves below its western end; and in all the rest of its course, the Thame seldom touches even a village. Oxfordshire folk know, too well, how flood-water hangs back in the levels; they build their cottages on any rise they can find above the water-meadows.

For the Thame gathers into the Thames the waters of a wide expanse of country. Its beginnings would be hard to trace up among the miles of rolling pasture that make up the Whaddon Chase country. Isolated hamlets, rural indeed, live their own life here, remote from railways or even from bus routes.

Quainton village, surrounded by grazing and cornland, is typical of this district. It has some grand farm buildings to please the connoisseur of massive barns; it has also the remains of a village cross and a windmill at the top of its green, and, along a side street, a gracious line of almshouses with an inscription recording their endowment in 1687—a picture of restfulness and quiet.

Quainton has maintained its own way of life for centuries. It was here that the villagers took their own line in the matter of the reform of the calendar. In 1753, when this country changed from the Julian to the Gregorian calendar,

DORCHESTER BRIDGE, OVER THE THAME WHERE IT JOINS THE THAMES.

the date had to jump forward eleven days to catch up the arrears of error resulting from the faulty calculations of Julius Cæsar's time and to accord with Pope Gregory's correction. Ardent Protestants put their feeling into the rhyme

" In seventeen hundred and fifty-three
The year was changed to Poperie ".

They held that they had been robbed of eleven days of life, and besieged Parliament with a clamour of " Give us back our eleven days ".

In Quainton they decided to test the matter for themselves. In the churchyard there grew a thorn-bush, claimed to be a shoot from the Holy Thorn of Glastonbury, which sprang from the staff that Joseph of Arimathea struck into the ground when, as west country tradition tells, he came to Britain and landed above the Severn shore at Glastonbury. That Holy Thorn was believed to flower at midnight on Christmas Eve. Quainton people devoutly believed that their thorn did the same, though few ever braved the midnight air to watch it bloom.

That winter, however, they decided to put their church's treasure to mundane use: they would let it decide the controversial question of dates. Accordingly they resolved to watch in the churchyard on the night of what the new calendar presumed to call Christmas Eve, though all up-holders of the old ways insisted that it was only the 13th of December.

They watched the thorn at midnight. There was not a sign of bloom. The good folk of Quainton returned home confirmed in their resistance to this new-fangled idea of changing the date. " The Thorn knew "; it wasn't Christmas, and they would continue to keep Old Christmas Day as the true and proper festival.

Whether any unbelievers watched also on the eve of Old

Christmas Day, no one is unkind enough to record. One would not like to think that the thorn was sterile on that night also; Quainton's faith in it continued unimpaired.

Anyone penetrating into North Bucks as far as Quainton might well take the opportunity, if the day should be clear and breezy and the going fairly dry, of walking up the slope of Quainton Hill behind the village. The view broadens out surprisingly, with cloud-shadows sweeping over other distant hills and across the wide levels of the vale, where many another village is to be found among these beginnings of the Thame.

Eastward from Quainton four miles of lane, up and down hill-slopes and over rivulets trickling southward, lead by Pitchcott to Whitchurch, which is less out of the world, being on the semi-main road from Aylesbury to Buckingham, with sixteenth-century timbered houses along its street and the ruins of Bolbec Castle—now little but a green mound—close by. A mile away across fields, and reached only by a private road from that Aylesbury–Buckingham highway, lies Creslow—simply manor-house and a few attendant cottages, with "Creslow Great Ground" stretching hedgeless into the distance towards another dip with another and a bigger stream, and a bigger rise beyond to the hunting country of Cublington and Aston Abbots. Anyone seeking a genuinely rural ride can trace the quadrangle of country road connecting those villages with Whitchurch and with Weedon. At the same time he will have penetrated reasonably near to the beginnings of the various streamlets and farm-brooks and watercourses that make up the Thame River. Starting hereabouts, twenty miles from the Thames, they take twice that distance to descend the couple of hundred feet which is their total fall in all their loops and windings.

This may account for the leisured unhurrying air of this

THE WINDMILL AND RUINED CROSS
ON THE VILLAGE GREEN, QUAINTON.

FINE OLD ALMS-
HOUSES, AND (*right*)
COBBLED PAVEMENT,
AT QUAINTON.

whole countryside; but herein lies a parable and a moral for the town-dweller, if he will observe the one and accept the other. Country life *is* unhurried, but that is because work and life follow a well-thought-out method. Absence of rush and flurry does not mean that things are not being done: rather the reverse. The farm labourer—whether cattle-man, tractor-driver, hedger, mechanized sheep-shearer, or all these things and much more as he often is—gets a great number of highly-skilled jobs done in his well-filled day, just as the River Thame does a great amount of work, both watering and draining a surprising number of farms, in the course of its peregrinations. It even has leisure to be ornamental as it skirts Eythorp Park. "Eethrup" joins on with Waddesdon—the great park around the Rothschild " chateau "—to form a fine stretch of wooded hillside.

A by-road with a sudden view across the vale towards the Chilterns, climbs southward from Waddesdon to the ridge-top hamlet of Upper Winchendon. More properly, this should be spoken of as Over Winchendon; its companion, Nether Winchendon, lies snugly down several lanes that branch to the left as this by-way continues along the ridge. It looks down on the little river threading its way among a group of villages; the lovely mellow stone of Nether Windendon Priory contrasts with the thatch and whitewash of Cuddington up the far slope; farther down the valley, the cottages, church, and rectory of Chearsley appear as a charming assembly as the road curves down among them and passes under railway and over rivulet, to begin a steep straight rise towards Long Crendon.

Path-finders may prefer to strike left here, where Notley Abbey lies down by the stream. The dovecot is a fine and unusual specimen, and the weathered stone of the old walls seems to defy the ages, even though the building

SOME FINE THATCHED COTTAGES IN LONG CRENDON.

material of 1162 has been incorporated in a modern dwelling. Haddenham, a village which in many ways resembles no other, lies ahead, up the ridge to the southward; but to reach it by road one may circle round by Long Crendon and Thame.

Both these places figure in later chapters, but no one will regret a second visit to either. Dwellings both old and new in Crendon seem to fit well into their surroundings, and its by-ways provide many a curious vista. Curious, too, is the phase in Crendon's history when it was a noted centre for needle-making, before the Redditch machine-made article made it revert to agriculture. A local booklet on the subject makes interesting reading.

Of even more interest is Thame, as Chapter Four will attempt to show. For the present it may suffice to observe the grand position of the church as one approaches it along the level road over Crendon Bridges and passes below its noble tower towards Priest End. The town can be left

NETHER WINCHENDON CHURCH, IN THE THAME VALLEY.

for more leisurely exploration; the church and its many fine monuments, too, could occupy a lengthy stay. But to continue village-wanderings: a footway leads conveniently by the church—almost a little " close " that gives something of a cathedral-town air. Actually, the collegiate church of Thame had considerable standing in the past.

This by-way connects with the Aylesbury road, which swings down, giving another fine view of the church, to cross another stream, for Thame marks the confluence of quite a number of tributaries into its own river. By the hamlet of Scotsgrove—an ancient toll-point, judging by the name—the road climbs to a fork where the left-hand way leads to Aylesbury and the right to the intriguing village of Haddenham.

At this fork, so local tradition goes, there was hanged the last man to be executed for sheep-stealing—the last in Thame, or in Bucks, or in England—the informant is never sure; but all story-tellers agree that the man was hanged only through another man calling " Baa-a-ah " after him. As to how this affected the issue, the stories differ once more. Either the " Baa-ee " killed his derider lest the latter should inform, and thus died for murder as well as for sheep-stealing; or the " Baa-er ", in fear of death, did inform. The one point on which all versions of the tale agree is that at this road-fork the last man to be hanged for sheep-stealing *was* hanged.

This legend of the gibbet can be left behind by taking either road. The left fork is the main road to Aylesbury, running high enough to look far away northward towards Chilton and Dorton—hamlets each dependent on the great house nearby. Along the valley below on the left, the Thame River winds among those villages of Chearsley and Cuddington and Nether Winchendon previously mentioned; this round trip is worth making to see the difference these villages present close at hand and from a distance. Cuddington can be visited by a turn left, at a point known locally as King's Cross, to rejoin this main road after a pleasantly rural couple of miles.

Cuddington, so entirely off the beaten track, is worth a visit to see various patterns of thatched roofs at its many turns and corners. It is also full of ancient legend, though the visitor may be puzzled by the local versions of history; to be told that Queen Anne sheltered here during the Wars of the Roses comes as a surprise if one thinks only of the Queen Anne who is remembered principally because she is dead. But that is not what Cuddington means. There is tradition, with possibly a slender foundation of fact, that during the Wars of the Roses, Anne Neville, daughter of Warwick the Kingmaker, did disappear from public view to escape the unwelcome attentions of Richard Crookback, Duke of Gloucester, and that she was found serving in

THAME CHURCH—
FULL OF INTERESTING
FEATURES, AND,
*below*, THE
CHURCH AND
COURT HOUSE
AT LONG CRENDON.

obscurity as a kitchen-wench. If that be true, what better spot for obscurity than Cuddington, even though, strictly speaking, she was not Queen Anne during her sojourn there, but only afterwards when Richard found her and persuaded her to be his queen?

Legend or no, Cuddington has individuality as a village, rural yet living and full of interest. So has Haddenham, which spreads out to cover a wide slope the other side of the Aylesbury road; it can be entered either from King's Cross or by the right-hand road from that gallows-corner above Scotsgrove.

This latter road, leaving the old mill of Scotsgrove below on the right, runs up for a straight mile and turns right, over the G.W. and L.N.E. mainline railway, with Haddenham church standing well up ahead. A magnificent solid and square Norman tower, and old pew-ends carved with agricultural emblems as befits a farming parish, make it a church not to be missed. One comes up the narrow, clay-walled approach-road to an open space of green extending right to the churchyard wall. Charming, well-kept old houses stand on either side; between them is one of Haddenham's many duck-ponds, for Haddenham is known far and wide as the place where they thatched over the pond to keep the ducks dry. Actually there is more practical sense in the tradition than in the jeer, for all knowledgeable duck-breeders agree that ducks should be kept dry—from rain—however much they swim. A more pointed local saying concerns the Haddenham man who bought a new wheelbarrow, and carried it home so as not to get the wheel dirty. This may be an aspersion as much on Haddenham mud as on Haddenham sense, for one peculiarity of the village is its building material, dug out of local pits.

This is a particularly sticky clay, known as " wychert ", which is kneaded with straw, and when built up into walls, by " shuttering " just as concrete is used, will dry solid and stand firm for years, provided it has a good coat of wash and is kept dry at top and bottom. For this reason, wychert walls are built on a brick or stone " footing ", and roofed with a ridge of tiles. Hence one finds these tiled walls, not only round gardens, but surrounding entire fields and " closes "; and their curves and angles, as the alley-ways between them wind about the village, make Haddenham a veritable maze to the stranger. It has been said to consist of " three ends and no middle ", parts of it being known in true Buckinghamshire fashion, as Church End, Town's End, and Fort End.

For all its peculiarities, Haddenham is a fascinating village. It was one of the last places to preserve the old English practice of open-field farming. This and many other memories of the village can be enjoyed in Walter Rose's *Village Carpenter* and *Good Neighbours*, where the true life of the old-time village is portrayed with a rare fidelity.

In this village, too, may be found several examples of country crafts still holding their own, though with difficulty, in face of changing conditions. One long-established firm of coach-builders pensioned off their oldest workman, and sought to instal an apprentice in his place.

That old man could make a waggon wheel. To comprehend fully what that means, one must not only read Walter Rose's illuminating account of the many processes involved, of the choice and shaping of the materials, of the strength and skill and judgment that go to such a work; but one must also see it done, and sense the artistry that times the operations and sees perfection taking shape. Such labour is art as well as craft.

It was no use. The young man got more money by joining the thousands at a nearby motor-car factory, and

A TYPICAL CORNER OF CUDDINGTON, ABOVE THE THAME RIVER.

spending his day driving in the screws of the hinges of the doors of the bodies of the cars.

However, Haddenham is a community with " life force " enough to survive. The village craftsmen find new products to employ their hereditary skill. Ladders and wheelbarrows and farm-gates are still in demand; portable buildings, poultry appliances, and many other essentials in wood and metal provide outlets for village enterprise, so that Haddenham can stand, and endure, as an example of the undying village community.

Beyond the open, breezy fields that slope away south and east from Haddenham, the wide level pastures of the Vale of Aylesbury stretch away to the Chilterns, and through

D

them, by Aston Sandford and Kingsey (both hamlets with fine old manor-houses visible from the road) there comes another little stream to swell the waters of the Thame River. It is a question whether the Vale of Aylesbury ought to be included in the country of the Thames. Aylesbury has decided views on most subjects, and feels that its Vale is its own; yet it owes a great deal of its fertility to the multitude of little streams that drain down to the Thame and the Thames, mostly by way of this brook that floods the Aston Sandford lane so thoroughly in winter. Scarcely a mile of the Chiltern hill-foot is without its spring bubbling from the Chalk, along the twenty-mile stretch from Britwell Salome in Oxfordshire to Cheddington and Aston Clinton away in Hertfordshire. Beyond that, the little streams a few miles away drain northwards into the Ouzel, which runs into the Ouse, which runs out by the Wash into the North Sea, through country very different from the Thames country to which this book must confine itself (though only by the exercise of firmness and sacrifice, as will be apparent at many points of the narrative). Barely 300 feet, the dividing rise of the ground towards the Hertfordshire–Bedfordshire border is enough to divert water, but not wind. The north-easterly breeze, refreshing in summer, but otherwise described at other times, blows uninterrupted by any hills in this quarter, and is one factor that makes the atmosphere of the Vale so noticeably fresher than that down-river.

Turn south-westward towards Thame, then—the metropolis of this Thame River area. A left turn beyond Kingsey avoids a dull straight three-mile rise, by a detour into Towersey—almost an island among those many streams that seek by devious ways to join the Thame.

A bold walker, or even a cyclist who flinches not at stiles or plank-bridges, might venture on a wider detour by

ONE OF HADDENHAM'S MANY DUCK-PONDS—THE HIGH STREET, AND FINE NORMAN CHURCH TOWER, OF HADDENHAM.

penetrating to Ilmer, or Illmire as non-residents characterize this lone hamlet. It lies down a lane that comes near to trespassing on Chiltern country, only a mile or two away, but Ilmer is unquestionably of the Vale. Only a few cottages and a couple of farms (yet lorry-loads of produce can be seen leaving for the London markets), it has the tiniest of churches, with unique mural carvings of very early date. Thence across meadows—drowsy in summer, but dank and dripping after any " weather "—the requisite sense of direction and a nose for the right path may bring a sight of the red roof and low grey pinnacles of Towersey church, surrounded by a medley of thatch and tile, with stout brick chimneys appearing above orchards and high hedges. Past the fine old hunting-box of Cotmore Wells, a straight mile or so of country road cuts across the rich acres of cultivation that surround the old town of Thame, where the entry into the spacious High Street brings the welcome sense of having discovered a country town indeed.

## CHAPTER FOUR

## A REAL COUNTRY TOWN

IT seems natural to speak of Thame as an old town. Old it certainly is, like so many other places which geographically make a centre for a wide circle of farms and villages. More than most towns of this kind, however, Thame has contrived to keep intact a number of the features that maintain the continuity of past and present.

The old houses down the High Street tell of prosperity and sound building—building both of dwellings and of fortunes. They convey a pleasing sense of dignified comfort—some creeper-covered, some with their fine stone mullions showing little sign of the wear of centuries. Professional brass plates display names familiar in the county, and in England, for generations; and round in a side street, over the yard of a coal, corn and seed merchant of the kind one finds in all country towns, there appears the modest legend " Founded in 1676 ".

Yet Thame is a town of the present as well, alive and up-to-date in its appreciation of current needs, as its fertilizer- and seed-suppliers, tractor depots, and radio shops testify. That old firm mentioned above can tell of the trains of horse-waggons loaded with poultry that set off for London before dawn; now modern lorries and milk-conveyors perform their services in less time but with the same reliability, for Thame and all this countryside plays its part in seeing that London is fed. Through the years, Thame preserves its own unhurried air.

This does not mean, though, that little is done here.

THAME MARKET IN PROGRESS.

As always in the country, and in the country town too, the business of life is transacted with order and dispatch. Through Thame market there passes a vast amount of livestock, whether under war-time conditions of " grading " (when a triumvirate of farmer, butcher, and auctioneer's valuer settle price and quality of all), or when pens of cattle, sheep, and pigs fill the whole of the upper High Street, and the auctioneer is king of the day. A wonderful sight is this gathering of stock, totalling thousands of pounds sterling and an inestimable sum in food-value; yet all is driven off and the street sluiced down by Tuesday evening, when Thame High Street reverts to its normal spacious leisureliness.

A number of particularly interesting buildings appear as one wanders through the town. Half-way down the High

Street, a quadrangle—town hall, shops, inns and houses of all shapes, sizes, and pitches of roof—nearly blocks its 190-ft. width. Down one side runs a narrow stone-paved Butter-market, on the other a roadway between hostelries of very diverse aspect. The number of inn signs visible in Thame, if one could count them all, would be eloquent witness to the demand for refreshment for man and beast from all the surrounding terrain, for which Thame forms such a focus. Two of the most notable face each other here. The " Spread Eagle ", whose emblem surmounts a massive post on the pavement, has been a celebrated house in many ways, as recorded by a former proprietor in his book *An Inn-Keeper's Diary*. Across the way from it, the " Birdcage " preserves handsome carved windowbays overhanging the ground floor, with still another storey overhanging again—one of the oldest houses in Thame. Serving as a house of correction during the Napoleonic Wars was only one incident in its history.

Lower down the High Street, Georgian, Queen Anne, and Elizabethan houses still survive. The old grammar school, not by any means new when the great John Hampden went there early in the 1600's, stands back in its own courtyard, an impressive mass of weathered stone. It was founded about 1575 by Lord Williams of Thame, whose home at Rycote, a few miles away towards Oxford, still stands in lovely grounds, which are occasionally open to the public. Sir John Williams, as he was in 1553, was one of the custodians of the Princess Elizabeth when on her way to confinement at Woodstock during the reign of her sister Mary. For the consideration he gave to her he was suitably rewarded when in due course she came into her own.

So one finds, down the street, all varieties of architecture harmonizing into a most attractive whole. Down at

THE SPACIOUS HIGH STREET OF THAME.

Priest End the street turns sharp left and right: left towards Oxford, past a striking example of timber, brick, and thatch; right, past the wall and entrance-lodge of one of the most attractive dwellings of all, the Prebendal. The weathered-stone, Cotswold-pattern tiles, and the Early English windows of the chapel are noteworthy, and a visit should be timed if possible for a day when the gardens are open, as happens occasionally with many local estates, for the benefit of nursing funds.

Thame church stands by the other side of this road, between two of the exits from the town, north-westward to Long Crendon, and north-eastward to Aylesbury. Its history, and that of the town, has been excellently detailed by several local writers. Anthony à Wood, the Oxford antiquary and a Thame man of Stuart times, has also recorded in his memoirs many incidents of his own and earlier days—notably, with glee befitting an ardent Royalist, the story of pies, baked under compulsion for the Roundheads, being enjoyed by Cavaliers who drove the Parliament troops out in the nick of time.

It seems right and proper to make a stroll round Thame a deliberate and leisurely affair, for the air of the place, though refreshing, does not invite hurry. Even crossing the street can be done without undue haste, for traffic has ample room; and that is as it should be, for the converging sides of the street show their medley of roofs and gables and cornices and porches to best advantage from the middle of the road. Thame can be included conveniently in a number of Thames-country tours, and every time one feels it is a pleasant place to visit.

For Thame is a friendly town. There, one never senses that repelling attitude of some country towns, which have a way of looking askance at " foreigners ". Thame goes its own way, and takes all as they come—whether it be one of the college cricket teams from Oxford, who will be sure of a keen game and the hospitality of the " Spread Eagle ", or a new resident, who will not be left long without an invitation to join the Bowls Club—with the assurance that " on the turf and under it, all men are equal ". Its cricket record, ranging from village matches to almost-county standard, is one of Thame's sources of pride, and it is an indication of how the game flourishes in this Minor County that a town of a few thousand inhabitants not only gives the colleges a good game but maintains three elevens. One way out of the town, when the time comes to leave it, passes the ground, where they now deplore the felling of the elms that W. G. Grace once hit a ball over. It certainly is a pity, for their height made the feat incredible to many;

though of course the natives thought it unnecessary to stress the point that the elms were not so high in W. G.'s time.

For a rural way back to the Thames, a by-way leaving the cricket ground on the right leads by a level-crossing over the single-track railway to Oxford, out of the town and into the fields at once. Something between a footpath and a cart-track, it winds between pasture and cabbage-fields, and over little bridges, into the hamlet of Moreton, a mile to the south. Timber-framed cottages—some neatly thatched, but a few sadly derelict—stand in their gardens round an up-to-date cemented farmyard—for agriculture moves with the times here. The way soon leaves Moreton behind, to follow a rising road, rough but fresh and breezy, up one of those low, ordinary little hills of South Oxfordshire which yet contrive to overlook a pleasing extent of country, with the Chiltern escarpment running dimly along on the left. Down into Tetsworth, where the great Oxford road sweeps through a cutting and the best of the village hides away round the church, with its short but graceful spire, the southward way continues. Up a steeper hill, those who fall victims to the fascination of Wittenham Clumps may look for a sight of them, beautiful as ever beyond the intervening rolling farmlands. Real country it is hereabouts, so wide-stretching that the townsman may feel himself " in the middle of nowhere "; yet to the observant eye there is abundant interest, if only agricultural interest, for there is infinite variety in that. The sight of an old-time " self-binder "—novelty of the 1890's—seems an anachronism in these days of up-to-date farming; but another field will be seen slashed with the great, deep furrows of the tractor-plough, and yet another will be dotted with neatly-baled hay where a fearsome-looking monster cuts and presses and ties, and throws out tons in an hour. The old and the new work side by side.

THE BIRDCAGE INN, ONE OF THAME'S OLDEST BUILDINGS.

Now all this, it may be protested, may interest a farmer (it doesn't, as a matter of fact, any more than a recital of the A.B.C. interests a poet or a Professor of English, for the present-day farmer's interests extend far deeper, to ·such matters as chemical soil-analysis, and the cellulose content of cornstalk), but surely there is more attraction for the tourist than these bucolics?   Certainly there is, first of all for the student of place-names.

Half-way up the rise to this hill-brow the map marks the hamlet of Stoke Talmage.   Now there are a great number of Stokes dotted about England, signifying usually the stockade of a Saxon landholder.   The curious point is that in many cases the " Stoke " part of the village-name forms the prefix to an unquestionably Norman surname. There is Stoke D'Abernon in Surrey, Stoke Damerell in Devon; in Somerset the well-known Stogumber and the less-known Stogursey were respectively Stoke de Gomer, and the Stoke of the great family of de Courcy.   Nearer home in the Vale of Aylesbury is Stoke Mandeville; and this Stoke Talmage was originally Stoke Tollemache, and any one who cares to delve into family histories will find records of this ancient name relating to this ancient hamlet.

THE VILLAGE OF GREAT MILTON, NEAR THAME.

For those more interested in seeing the beauties of the country, there is a massive thatched and weather-boarded barn, with golden lichen covering even the slates of the adjoining cartshed, standing grandly at the corner where the lane to Stoke Talmage leaves this upward road; and the church with a small tiled steeple-gable can be seen above the few roofs that surround it.

This stretch of country was not always so unpeopled as it is now. Within a few miles of the crossroad at Clare Hill, traces can be found in various fields and lanes of four ruined manor-houses, buildings of considerable size and importance, judging from the dimensions of the green mounds. These may some day tempt the amateur antiquary. For the present, the impatient cycle- or motor-tourer may be thankful that the two miles south-south-west from Clare Hill are a quick and easy downhill run, for it must be conceded that it is two miles without a single habitation, down to Cut Mill, which is still a mill though its mill-stream is only a sluggish trickle. Let it be stressed, however, that no real country can be one solid mass of the picturesque or the antique. It takes quite a number of acres of farmland to produce sustenance for the population of any one acre of town; and unless this country is to become one continuous Slough Trading Estate, one must accept the broad acres of cultivation, and thank heaven for the view ahead and the luxuriant hedgerows on both sides.

However, one would not inveigle the tourist who does not happen to be a hunting man into traversing the South Oxfordshire country, unless there were something for him to see beyond ridge-and-furrow and well-layered hedges. Just ahead there is interest in plenty.

At Cut Mill road-junction one may wonder whether to bear right for Chalgrove—historical interest is there, certainly, in the Hampden Monument to the historic

THE OLD MILL AT HOLTON.

skirmish of 1643—or to zigzag on towards Brightwell Baldwin—inviting-sounding name—or to digress into Cuxham, where a road winds away to Watlington and the Chilterns.

Sometimes inspiration comes at such moments, and whispers " Have a look at Cuxham "; and in this case it is right.

Cuxham (" Cooks'm " to all who live there and all who know it) is one of those villages blessed with a little stream running alongside the street. Timbered- and thatched-cottages make up that curving street—some are isolated, one long row has a generous overhang to the eaves, and a round-roofed one is set in a garden full of colour. Like all true cottage-gardens this one is packed with rose bushes, growing among annuals and perennials without any apparent formal plan, yet looking just right; for cottagers have a sense, handed down for generations, that some plants

" don't go with " others, so they are never planted together.

Beyond the low stone wall by the brook, and through a thin line of fir trees, the little stone tower of the church shows its tiled turret. The village street curves on, past a farmyard with a muddy track beyond, which one can follow in search of one of those long-vanished manor-houses previously mentioned, though of this the village has scarcely a memory. A little alley-way leads back to the church, past a building with a most beautifully tiled roof and fine brick chimney-stacks—a tiny school with climbing plants in profusion up its walls. Close by stands the church, at first glance an ordinary village church, until the west doorway at the foot of the tower is seen to be flanked by spiral-carved stone pillars with ornamented capitals; and in the round Norman archway itself, both outside and in, are traces—despite age and restoration— of threefold chevron ornamentation. Some of the old oak pews still remain, and in the floor is a fine brass of John Gregory of Cuxham, with his two wives, five sons, and one daughter all portrayed wonderfully clearly considering its age, for the date shows as 1506, while a wall-tablet tells of another Gregory of 1688. This is a country church which it is a joy to find.

Brightwell Baldwin, a mile to the west, has a bigger church, standing above the few well-kept cottages that fringe Brightwell Park. The " Lord Nelson ", whose brightly-coloured sign catches the eye, has some curious ornamentations and carvings, of all apparent ages, on wall and doorposts. The magnificent avenue of cedars forming one entrance to the Park, and the stone eagles over another, indicate a great house with a past. But one is soon through Brightwell and away again over country of smooth, rounded hillocks, towards a village which could fill a chapter by itself—Ewelme.

PART OF CHALGROVE VILLAGE STREET, NOT FAR FROM THAME.

Ewelme is a place impossible to do justice to in a short description or a single visit. One must return there again and again to absorb the beauty and the interest, first of the church with its many historical associations and its wonderful carvings, then of the quadrangle of alms-houses adjoining it, and then of the setting of the village, where the character of the country begins to change from those easy-sloping cultivated fields of the vale to the sharper outlines of the chalk hills. It is a place where lingering is doubly justified, for beyond it, towards the Thames, the swelling rises of hill-foot grow barer and steeper, as though the land had thrown up bigger and less friendly waves. They grow harsher and chalkier, too, with not even a hedge breaking the sweep of a mile and more of flinty plough-land. A townsman, hurrying homeward, with the mist of a late afternoon making the Berkshire Downs across the river look distant and mountainous, might well feel, in this curiously contrasting country between the wooded slopes of Goring and the pleasant fields of the Thame, that he had indeed strayed into the middle of nowhere.

Suppose, on the other hand, that a detour westward from Cut Mill had been made—*after* visiting Cuxham, for that is a digression not to be neglected. Again the road curves pleasantly by a brook-edged, wide-stretching sweep of farm-land; bramble and willow-herb give the authentic rural touch, until, round a bend, there looms what at first glance seems a dark, distant mountain. At second glance it is seen to be not so very distant, but still dark and huge— one of the immense hangars of Chalgrove airfield. Ancient and modern stand cheek by jowl here with a vengeance, for at the very entrance—a forbidden entrance—of this up-to-date aerodrome there stands, still and modest, a stone obelisk within iron railings.

THE QUADRANGLE OF THE ALMS-HOUSES AT EWELME.

E

The inscription gives the name " JOHN HAMPDEN ".
It reads:—

> Within a few feet of this spot, he received the wound of
> which he died while fighting in defence of the free monarchy
> and the ancient liberties of England, July, 1643.

This expresses the sentiments of Hampden and of many
other stalwarts of the Parliamentary forces in the Civil
War. The monument speaks eloquently though silently
of the enduring quality of this English countryside, which
has changed little in the three centuries since it made such
ideal ground for the cavalry tactics of both Rupert and
Hampden.

The present writer was once waiting, with camera set up,
for the sun to come out from behind a cloud, when a car
came along the then open road—now the airfield—and
stopped at sight of the monument. The occupants got
out to investigate, all except one who remained seated and
called out an inquiry as to " what it was all about ". The
answer came that " it seemed to be something to do with
history ".

History! History comes to life here at Chalgrove,
where the road leads away westward to Chiselhampton
Bridge—the only bridge in the ten miles between Wheatley
and Dorchester where Prince Rupert's men could re-cross
the Thame River to regain Oxford. It was across these
same fields northward that John Hampden turned his
horse to find succour in Thame when he knew his wound
had put him out of the fight. The story tells that it was the
effort of jumping the Haseley Brook, then as now meander-
ing westward to join the Thame, that re-opened the wound
and made it indeed mortal, for he died at the house of
Ezekiel Brown, physician—which still stands, though now
a shop, at the foot of that narrow little Butter-market of
Thame, noticed earlier in this chapter.

THE CHURCH OF ST. HELEN, AT ABINGDON.

John Hampden belongs more properly—except that he belongs to all England historically—to the Chilterns than to the lowlands, though he had associations with both Sydenham and Pyrton, nearer the hill-foot. Each of these villages has more " history " for the historically minded. For those seeking the charm of out-of-the-way villages several routes are at hand.

Half a mile south from the monument, a turn right leads along the mile of scattered inns and dwellings that form Chalgrove village, where apple and pear trees overhang the houses, and the big, pinnacled tower of the church stands down by the brook. Keeping westward the road leads through Stadhampton and on to Chiselhampton by the same little stone bridge that was so vital to Prince Rupert. Both villages have narrow, sharp-angled streets round their thatched cottages; and thence there is a main road, or by-roads with more digressions, towards the " works " of Cowley.

If southward from Chalgrove is the direction for the day, there is still choice of route to rejoin the main road by the Thames. Another turn right can reach Drayton St. Leonard, by ford or footbridge across the Thame, with two miles to go to Dorchester.

To reach the Thames nearer Benson or Wallingford, however, the southward road holds on through Berrick Prior. It looks a village worth exploring, but one wonders where; there seems so little of it on the map. It may happen, at the right time, that one hears the sound of bells across the fields, particularly mellow bells, and again one wonders, where?

The map shows a church, but no road to it. The only way is to follow the sounds of the bells down a side-track that seems to lead into a farmyard; but another track bends round leftward, curves, and forks—and still no church is visible, though the bells sound near—and the track ends at a hedge and stile just in front. It is only on passing a huge chestnut tree that one sees, completely screened by it, a little church that is truly beautiful. It has a venerable timbered porch, a gold-and-brown weathered roof, and a tiny tower varied by tiers of stone, tile, and fine open timber-work, with a massive wooden cross on the summit of its tiled gable. In its setting of fields and hedges, this church of Berrick Prior is another of the gems of this countryside.

Southward still, Berrick Salome, Roke, and Rokemarsh string their cottages along this road almost continuously down to Benson. There, one turns into a fine old street of substantial houses and many inns, before picking up the arterial highway; one must be prepared, hereabouts, for the liberties modern construction has taken with Ordnance map roads since the last revision. South-eastward still, the Reading road skirts the immense expanse of Benson airfield, where the flare-path straddles even the main road.

Gazing across a mile and more of once fertile country at the gaunt curves and angles of shelters and hangars, one may wonder whether the peacefulness of cultivation and quiet growth has been banished hence for ever. Kipling wrote a story once, called " The Bridge-Builders ". They built a bridge that should endure; and though it withstood flood and tempest, in the eyes of the gods of river and plain it was a thing of a moment.

So, possibly, it may be with the hangars and runways of Benson and Chalgrove. For

> " while the earth remaineth, seed-time and harvest, and cold and heat, and summer and winter, and day and night, shall not cease ".

## CHAPTER FIVE

# OXFORD'S COUNTRY

THE little River Thame that rises in the little hills of north Buckinghamshire traverses, as has been seen, a stretch of country really rural yet within easy reach of London. In another hour's journey westward by road or rail, bigger rivers come down from the bigger hills of the Cotswold and the Northamptonshire upland; but before they claim too much attention, one may well notice a tract of country, between the beginnings of the Thame and the beginnings of Cotswold, that seems to centre naturally upon Oxford.

The City and University of Oxford as such are beyond the scope of this book. The influence of Oxford on the Thames is the influence of a city and of a university; yet Oxford is also, among its other aspects, a country town, whose folk like to enjoy the country that encircles them, and whose countryfolk are drawn to Oxford as their metropolis. This particularly applies north-eastward, where no towns such as Abingdon or Witney or Woodstock form counter-attractions.

Quainton Hill was noticed in Chapter Three as the limit of Thames country, since beyond its 500-ft. brow the streams begin to run away from the Thames towards Bedfordshire. Farther westward, the watershed is far less discernible, not even reaching 300 feet; and field follows field—rich grazing ground—for mile after mile towards Bicester, one of the few towns in southern England from which hardly a hill can be seen. That fact probably operated in its favour as a site for airfields, of which it has abundance; and—a good point in the eyes of those employed at airfields—roads and railways in all directions make Bicester an easy place to get away from.

Roads have radiated from Bicester since very early times. The great Roman Akeman Street, making for Bath, came straight from Aylesbury to the station of Alchester, a mile south of Bicester, to slant away to Ciren-cester (Corinium of the Dobuni) across the Cotswold foot-hills. At Alchester it was crossed by the south-to-north Roman way from Dorchester and the Thames crossing below Sinodun, heading towards Towcester on the still greater Watling Street that ran on to Chester. The rail-ways, too, found easy going hereabouts, and in the first two miles westward from Quainton, by a gated road through open fields, one finds three great main lines sweeping across country with little to stop for. The villages for the most part lie away from both railway and main roads, and those most worth visiting can be found by discriminating rambles along the by-ways.

One such is Grendon Underwood, westward still from Quainton. It verges on the Akeman Street but keeps its most characteristic features to itself along its own side lane. Grendon is alleged to have given Shakespeare the material from which he drew the immortal Dogberry in *Much Ado About Nothing*, but whether from any authentic village constable it is not recorded. It is claimed that Grendon formed the half-way house between Stratford and London where Shakespeare stayed; and Grendon remains a village which Shakespeare and many another may have enjoyed visiting. So does Stratton Audley, some five miles on by a country road that misses Bicester and wanders through Marsh Gibbon instead, though in doing so it leaves many loops and quadrangles of Marsh Gibbon's winding streets unvisited except by confirmed digressors.

Stratton Audley, however, though a village of distinctive character, lies very near the boundary of the Thames country, and more typical villages can be found southward from Grendon Underwood. Ludgershall has interest as well as charm, for John Wyclif was once rector there. "Luggers'l" lies pleasantly along and between two diverging roads southward. The left-hand one curls round the edge of Wotton Park by a blind lane to the hamlet of Wotton Underwood—"Wood-town under the Wood"—truly so called, for it is quite overshadowed by its great house and park. The other branch, or leg, of Ludgershall village bears upward towards Brill, of which more later, for an interesting and, in some ways, unique patch of country lies westward.

Cross the railway, then the county boundary—whether one notices it or not, local patriots on either side aver that you can tell by the improvement in the road surface—then a by-road where Piddington village strings out to right and left, and then another, semi-main, road from Thame to Bicester. Keeping westward still, the by-way climbs over a little ridge, with oak woods fringing the roadside and gates to open here and there, passes Lower Arncot almost without noticing that also, and zigzags towards a

RIVERSIDE MEADOWS NEAR BENSON CHURCH.

THE FINE CHURCH TOWER OF BICESTER.

village that is worth a pause to view it from the river-meadows by the roadside.

The map and the signposts call it Ambrosden, but that naturally becomes " Ammersden " locally. The massive church tower stands magnificently among the fine timber flanking it, with the roofs of well-built farm-steadings completing the picture. The road turns sharp left on entering the village, and by following it one can begin to trace a circle, or rather the five-mile sides of a rough square, around the curious expanse of Otmoor.

Even before it became a bombing-ground, one usually had to go round Otmoor. The only way right across it was a track along the line of that old Roman road running northward to Bicester. Even that was passable only after a long spell of dry weather, for Otmoor is simply a huge shallow bowl of almost perfectly flat marsh. The colouring of a contoured map shows clearly what a drainage-basin this level is bound to be. A circle three to four miles across has the faint but decisive 200-ft. mark ringing it round completely, except for the Islip outlet, where the little River Ray that has percolated in from the north and gathered tributary brooklets literally from all directions creeps through to join the Cherwell.

With all this drainage-in, it is easy to see what a waste Otmoor is bound to be. Even after that dry spell that made it possible with pains and pertinacity to follow the old track from Beckley up to Alchester, past Joseph's Stone—a former Roman mile-post by the wayside—an expanse of tall grass and bents, rank weeds, scrub, and low-spreading bushes stretched away on all sides, alive with bird and insect life. After rain, spongy swamp and stagnant pools appeared immediately, and Otmoor became as impenetrable to the stranger as it must have been in earlier ages.

It would be wrong to say that no one could traverse

THE VILLAGE CHURCH OF GRENDON UNDERWOOD.

Otmoor at any time and in any weather, because the folk who live round its fringes have for generations been almost a race apart. They know its moods as well as they know the ways—hardly even tracks—that provide sure and safe going; but that knowledge is not for outsiders. They gained their livelihood, by hook or by crook, from the wild itself, or from their cultivable patches round its rim and the five towns of Otmoor. Ferncot, Oddington, Noke, Beckley, and Studley—with sundry other claimants for the distinction who sought to oust one of these—pursued their own way of life and formed almost a league, a close corporation of their own governing; and Otmoor, so far as its neighbourhood can be visited, still forms an island of as really primitive country as any in the island of Britain.

The little ridge above-mentioned, as one leaves the scrubby oakwood between Upper and Lower Arncot, forms one slight eminence high enough to give a view over the northern part of Otmoor. So, from the south, does the edge of the higher ground north of Beckley, where cornfields end and the wild scabious flourishes amazingly. So also, at gaps here and there, does the lane that turns westward by the great barn-like blacksmith's shop at the corner of Studley hamlet, to reach out towards Horton; but,

> " To Horton-cum-Studley
> The road's wet and puddly "

has been a saying for many years among rival villages; and in a voyage of discovery, from Ambrosden above the northern bounds of Otmoor round to Boarstall beyond the eastern edge, one may find many of the roads shown on the map to be impassable, whether on account of the nature of Otmoor or of warning notices of " Danger ".

John Buchan, before he became Lord Tweedsmuir and had no more time for writing thrillers of past days in the intervals of making history so readable, had a fondness for Otmoor and the mysterious life that flourished round its borders. *The Blanket of the Dark* tells of the painted floor at Beckley, where the mosaic pavement of a Roman villa was well-known in Tudor times. And in several other romances that master-hand has peopled this lost territory with the secret societies of masterless men who harboured hereabouts. It is a fascinating and surprising section of this countryside, so near Oxford and yet so different from the districts round it.

Eastward from Otmoor the ground rises more sharply, culminating in the isolated height of Brill. On the way there is Boarstall hamlet, which has a fine reminder of the past in the tower that stands beyond the moat, still inhabited, and the sole relic of a great house, ancient enough to have been castellated by the authority of King John, and so strong and important that it withstood siege in the Civil War. The tower now standing was actually only the gate-

BRILL WINDMILL, ON ITS HEIGHT OUTSIDE THE VILLAGE.

house of that castle, formerly the home of the custodian of the royal forest of Bernewood that covered many miles of this countryside in Plantagenet times.

Now, after centuries of the ups and downs of farming, Boarstall and Oakley and Worminghall are the village centres for scattered farms of many acres. Mostly it is grazing land in the gently-sloping meadows between the many brooks that find their devious ways southward, though sometimes cultivation, under the spur of a War Agricultural Executive Committee—the farmers' own blend of democracy-bureaucracy—calls up memories of the past: on one farm the mole-plough, cutting deep to drain the moisture that hangs in this heavy land, unearthed earlier and deeper drainage-pipes, so early and so deep that their outlet into the brook was a foot beneath its present bed. Such is the volume of sediment deposited, within probably a single century, by one insignificant streamlet. Multiply the century by scores, and the stream by hundreds, and one begins to realize the work that all Thames water has been doing throughout the river's history, in laying down the market gardens and nursery beds of the lower valley.

One of the most self-sufficient villages within the Thames orbit is Brill, which stands on its own hill overlooking Boarstall and Oakley. Much of the village is some 550 feet above sea-level—the highest ground in Bucks apart from the Chilterns—and the isolation of its height gives it a wide and variegated prospect. The inhabitants declare that from its adjoining summit of Muswell Hill, the ordnance surveyors, when they set up their observing tower there, could clearly see the coast of France.

Anyone who cares to do so can test this claim by drawing a contour-profile on a line from Brill to Boulogne. Certainly an observer stands a better chance of seeing France from here than from Muswell Hill, N.W. if clearness of atmosphere can help. The winds that blow round Brill have well served the ancient windmill on the open plateau beyond the village, and the freshness of the air makes a climb hither a real tonic.

The Thame road south-eastward down the long " tail " of Brill Hill leads into one of the most attractive villages of the district. Long Crendon has an unusual number of thatched houses—solid, well-kept cottages and inns; it has an air of spaciousness set off by its situation on the brow of a hill dropping sharply to the Thame river. Eastward too, beyond the lovely fifteenth-century timbered Court-house, a by-road leads down towards Chearsley and its companion villages in the valley. Westward, beyond the fine stone entrance-arch of the manor-house, another lane

THE RIVERSIDE
WOODS AT
NUNEHAM, BELOW
OXFORD.

POPLARS IN THE
PARKS AT
OXFORD.

winds down and down to discover the hamlet of Shabbington, where a few secluded cottages and a church with a
massively buttressed tower cluster round a bend of the
river.

Farther on towards Oxford, Ickford stands up in the
open away from the river—a village of character that gives
the impression of knowing what is worth doing and doing
it well, for the gardens, and the signs of local activities,
mark it as a place of enterprise. The river winds on,
through meadows with deep grass and great hedges of oak
and elm; it leaves on one side Waterstock and on the other
—within hail but five miles away by road—Waterperry,
where inter-village cricket matches provide gossip for after
years. " Go on, you're out," said the home umpire when a
visiting big-hitter ridiculed a leg-before decision, " Y're
'ittin' too blimmin' 'ard."

So the Thame goes winding among its villages, every
one different and most of them with some feature that will
make a pleasant memory. Thame and Thames are only
some four miles apart here, but both have long courses to
follow still before they unite at Dorchester. Meanwhile,
just a mile or so the other side of Oxford, there lie other
types of country that are different again.

Among ways of reaching the other side of Oxford the
" By-pass " is one of the speediest, but it is an example
of how arterial highways seem to discover uninteresting
country. The other main road, by Headington, soon
becomes suburban; but there is a road-fork at Wheatley,
below the church and a block of fine stone-built cottages,
where what begins as the low road soon becomes the high
road over Shotover Hill. In actual fact it was the high
road of coaching days, and at the beginning of the long run
down to Magdalen Bridge it used to provide a view-point
from which the many spires of Oxford could be seen as they

F

deserve. Now, growth of trees and, latterly, the spread of building make the view sadly elusive.

A road branching still farther left from Wheatley, however, finds a village green still at Horsepath—one of the few villages that look pretty even from the railway. Beyond there, the mazes of Cowley may be threaded by aiming steadily for Littlemore station, and a mile beyond the railway a by-road to the right strikes the river at Sandford.

One of the surprises of Sandford is the immense depth of the lock. Another is the rapid change from industry to woods and fields; the southward road to Abingdon, past Radley, is delightfully tree-lined and shady.

Abingdon may be visited now or later, or any number of times; its interest is inexhaustible. Another good way to approach it—for the cyclist—is a detour to Cumnor, up on the hill to the right, thence taking advantage of the four-mile, gentle run-down by Wootton, with the far-away Berkshire Downs forming a sky-line to the south.

There are many other ways diverging from Cumnor, however. The main interest of Cumnor is the semi-historical one of Cumnor Place, though its site can throw no fresh light on the mystery of Amy Robsart as related in *Kenilworth*. The village inn, however, maintains the name of the " Bear and Ragged Staff "; it has a massive stone outside-chimney, and the many thatched cottages are attractive individually, though Cumnor as a village does not strike one as presenting the picture of unity that some other villages do.

A way that leads to distinctly different type of country is the road by Bessels Leigh down to Fyfield and Kingston Bagpuze. It is Thames country, unquestionably, for the river itself is only a couple of miles away on the right, where Longworth and Hinton Waldrist reach down to it by lanes from their back doors; but just here the dominant

WEATHER-VANE AT
KINGSTON BAGPUZE.

THE NORMAN CHURCH,
AND CROSS IN
CHURCHYARD, AT
IFFLEY.

impression one has is that this is the way to the West.
The Vale of White Horse is beginning to assert itself on the
left, and the road seems to invite one to hurry on along the
rising ridgelet towards Faringdon, to catch the first sight
of the White Horse of Wessex away across the Vale.    Beyond Faringdon the signposts point to Swindon, and Swindon also conjures up visions of the G.W.R. and its expresses
to the West.    So it may be well to hark back to Cumnor
for another and more leisurely route to the Upper Thames
Valley.

Leisurely is the right word for the most direct way from
Cumnor down to the river.    Walkers can make almost a
straight line of it, westward by the Long Leys; roadfarers
drop gently to Eaton and then strike steeply down to river
level; but both arrive inevitably at the place that is, above
all others, both Thames and country—the celebrated ferry
of Bablock-hithe.

It is impossible not to refer to Matthew Arnold's " Scholar
Gipsy " here.    He mentions several of the features of this
Oxford country; for the most part those mentions prove
the rule, that English proper names are not poetical in
sound, perhaps through the severely practical habit of
modifying them so that they come trippingly off the tongue.
Sutton, for instance, can never make poetry, though the
" South Town " that it signifies might.    Yet here is the
exception—this name of three ugly syllables which together
contrive to make music.

" Crossing the stripling Thames at Bablock-hithe," sings
Arnold; and to appreciate the picture that is conjured up
by the words one must come here and be pulled gently
across to the shady peaceful meadows into which one steps
from the ferry.

The Thames is a fairly hearty stripling here, though
narrower by far than the majestic river only a few miles

STANTON HARCOURT CHURCH, NEAR THE FERRY OF BABLOCK-HITHE.

away across the Oxford loop, between Iffley and Sandford. Iffley, by the way, deserved a detour before leaving that side of Oxford; the Norman church is a lovely example of solid yet beautiful building, and its position enjoys the quiet country outlook of this famous rowing reach.

From Iffley to Bablock-hithe in a straight line is only six miles. By river it is nearly twice that distance, during which the Thames receives the very considerable tribute of the Cherwell and the Evenlode, as well as the overflow of the Duke of Marlborough's lake in Woodstock Park. All those additions together, however, can hardly account for the complete change in character of the River Thames between those two places. One can put it down only to its passage through Oxford; no one can experience that and be unchanged.

Up-river from Bablock-hithe, then, the river will be found to be a real country stream. One of its most typical villages lies just inland from the ferry, reached by a lane, winding back between hedges with lofty elms, which comes suddenly on the imposing towers of Stanton Harcourt manor-house.

This has been the residence of the Harcourt family since at least Norman times. A part of the building now in use dates from 1250. One tower still standing—one of the original four at the corners of the huge quadrangle—is "Pope's Tower" with a room at the top where the poet translated part of his great work the *Iliad*. Memories of Pope are in the church, too, including an epitaph he wrote on two lovers struck by lightning.

Most of the memorials in Stanton Harcourt church, especially those in the Harcourt chapel, are naturally connected with the Harcourt family. There is an effigy of the Harcourt who was Henry the Seventh's standard-bearer at Bosworth; there is the Simon Harcourt of Queen Anne's time; and a Lady Harcourt is shown wearing the ribbon of the Garter. The church has other points of interest in the Norman arches of its doorways and the nine lancet windows of the chancel, beautiful in their plain Early English simplicity.

The village has some interesting cottages also, especially one with a long, thatched roof with six dormer windows in a row; and when the time comes to finish exploring the many corners and winding ways of Stanton Harcourt, routes can be chosen in whatever direction suits the purpose. South and west lies the main river, with its villages keeping away from its flood waters by a cautious mile or two. West and north one can try to trace the many waters that here form the bifurcations of the Windrush—an unusual geological phenomenon, which those interested may care to

THE WINDING THAMES
AND (*below*) SWINFORD
BRIDGE AT EYNSHAM.

*Left :* THE WINDRUSH
AT MINSTER LOVELL.

ponder. Alternatively, a winding lane leads northward to Eynsham for a return to Oxford if that suits, by way of Swinford Bridge, where the river seems to be growing perceptibly bigger as it sweeps looping through the meadows and the bridge has to take long strides to cross. " Ensh'm " is not at first sight a prepossessing little town, and has had its ups and downs, even in recent years. Having been a junction of many by-roads with the Gloucester highway, it is short-circuited by the by-pass; it had a brief agricultural distinction due to its sugar-beet factory; but it improves with acquaintance, and has the freshness in its atmosphere that one finds in such wide level stretches as this.

Here, as at Stanton Harcourt, the question arises, not only which route to choose, but which branch of the river is the next to explore, and it may be expedient to cast a comprehensive eye over the streams that blend hereabouts to see what contribution each of them makes to the Thames.

## CHAPTER SIX

## AROUND THE HEADWATERS

THE bigger hills previously mentioned, which give rise to bigger rivers as one traces the Thames farther westward, include the Cotswold ridge, where several of the tributaries rise well back towards the 800-ft. escarpment, and also the rather bleak hill-country of the Warwickshire–Northamptonshire border. Anything like a real " beating-of-the-bounds " of the Thames and all its subsidiaries would therefore lead well into the Midlands and the West Country.

The northern tributaries begin as those discriminating trickles of water which decide to run southwards, i.e., towards the sun, rather than towards those dreary Midlands which Mr. Belloc has stigmatized as " sodden and unkind ". Without displaying partisanship, one may commend their good sense, for an outstanding characteristic of the Thames is that it is a happy river.

This applies not only to the multitude who find their fun in it, on it, or beside it, in their leisure. Talk to the lock-keepers, boat-builders, mill-workers—even to the few surviving toll-bridge keepers—up and down its length, and thank heaven for the river's cheering influence on all whose work is connected with it. Carry the experiment a stage further by contact with the riverside farmers, villagers, town tradesmen; taking them by and large, and allowing for the exception that proves every rule, it will be found that the visitor is welcomed—provided that he himself is similarly actuated—as a fellow-being with complementary interests who can learn from the countryman, and from whom, possibly, the countryman may also learn.

Whether that attitude extends beyond the southern chalk hills into Mr. Belloc's own south country is a question beyond the scope of this book. It holds good in those Thames-side parts of Berkshire and Wiltshire which will be explored in due course. If those explorations should penetrate the chalk rampart and discern the same characteristics prevailing there also, that will provide one more proof of the pervasive cheerfulness of Thames philosophy, and at the same time an instance of the difficulty of setting hard and fast limits to any subject connected with the Thames.

A tour of the northern watershed could be done more easily on the map than on the ground. It is only here and there that a road happens to follow the dividing ridge, and the streamlets overlap and interlace in a way difficult enough to follow on paper; and it was seen in Chapter Three how slight an elevation may be enough to rob Thames and enrich Ouse.

Farther west, the convolutions of such an imaginary journey would be even more involved. It would have to do some very careful circling round Stratton Audley, where the headwaters of the Buckingham-bound Ouzel drive it almost into the very valley of the Cherwell, right to the old track that runs northward along the crest behind Upper Heyford. It could swing away again over the great " Aynho Cut " of the Great Western Railway, to throw a big loop around the Souldern and Croughton valleys (where the lowland is much more inviting than the upland). It could not be allowed to visit Hinton-in-the-Hedges, but might be permitted to investigate Farthinghoe; and, after steering carefully over the Banbury–Brackley–Towcester railway junction, it would, very regretfully, have to leave on its right one of the most interesting of all English

OLD MILL ON THE WINDRUSH
AT COKETHORPE, NEAR WITNEY.

THE SIGN OF THE " BEAR AND
RAGGED STAFF ", AT FENNY COMPTON.

THE MANSION OF COMPTON
WYNYATES.

country-houses—Sulgrave Manor, the home of George Washington's ancestors. Up here, and on towards the maze of railways around Byfield and Woodford—whence it is possible, by some line or other, to reach almost any place in England—the impression of the Midlands grows noticeably stronger, and one feels that circumambulating the many little confluents of the Cherwell is leading quite far enough northward.

A cut across the Upper Cherwell valley can be made by taking the Banbury road south-west through Wardington, as far as a single-arm signpost that points to Williamscot. A single-arm signpost is often an excellent guide. This one leads in a few yards to a line of cottages—thatched, with stone mullions round the lead-framed windows. Beyond Williamscot a road slants gently down—an avenue, really, of lime and plane trees through which the tower of Cropredy Church appears beyond river and canal. Here is the famous Cropredy Bridge, where Cavalier and Roundhead cavalry met in one of the early engagements of the Civil War; Stuart-period armour has been dug up in the fields close by. Now, Crup'dy rests on its past, lying quietly up the slope with little canal traffic to disturb it. Temple Thurston's *Flower of Gloucester* tells a delightful tale of a canal-boat voyage through this peaceful valley. Up beyond Cropredy a winding lane by Mollington crosses the ridge between the Cherwell and a parallel valley westward. The lane curves on, up this second valley; it is wide and shallow and gently-rising, with luxuriant woodland up the slopes, which steepen as the way approaches the valley-head. A sharp bend leftward, and one comes all at once on a scene of beauty: Warmington village climbs up the hillside, where a Tudor manor-house looks down over the green, with magnificent walnut trees up the slope behind it. The top of that slope is the beginning of the top of Edge

Hill, so that this short cut has decidedly reached the bound of Thames country.

Suppose, however, the Cherwell were followed round its most northerly sources after all; it would be found to have decided affinities with the Thames even there. Also, the " Oxford Canal ", with its neat little tip-up foot-bridges which respond readily to the weight of a man, but keep cattle effectively within bounds, continues its placid way northward. Its route to the Midlands chooses the same gap that two railways have found the easiest, towards Fenny Compton station, where horse-boxes still form a fair proportion of the traffic and the Midland levels begin in earnest.

By this time, the tour of the watershed is definitely bear-ing southward towards Edge Hill, for the Burton Dasset windmill, standing out on its isolated knoll beyond the end of the plateau, is an outpost of the Stratford Avon, well beyond the routes of Thames tourists.

It is doubtful whether Edge Hill should be permitted in the south-westward tour from here: it is the actual water-shed, true, but such attractions as Compton Wynyates, and the Red Horse of Tysoe, might lead one far away from Thames territory.

Any such journey as this round the heads of all these sub-rivers would obviously run grave danger, not of degener-ating, but of developing, into a thoroughgoing Cotswold tour. One must discriminate firmly between what does and what does not appertain to the Thames.

On in the Cotswold proper such discrimination is easier. The watershed would lead to the Rollright Stones; but they are indisputably Cotswold, not Thames at all. So is Chipping Norton—a genuine ridge-side town—though Great Tew, eastward, with its big-built cottages looking away towards the Cherwell, belongs to the valley. One can be guided only by that undefinable something called the " feel of the country ", and turn towards home when it seems to be growing less characteristic of the Thames.

Among the Cotswold tributaries, especially, there are many of these fine variations of character. Take the Evenlode, as far up as Adlestrop; an express train once " drew up there unwontedly " and inspired Edward Thomas to write that what he saw

> " Was Adlestrop—only the name
>
> And willows, willow-herb, and grass,
> And meadowsweet, and haycocks dry,
> No whit less still and lonely fair
> Than the high cloudlets in the sky."

Those lines could apply only to a stretch of river-country; herein Evenlode has a link with Thames, thirty miles away down the long sweeping curves of its valley. Yet the Windrush valley is so completely Cotswold that it is doubtful if Thames ought to claim any of it above Minster Lovell.

Coln and Churn, too, are purely Cotswold in their valleys, as Leach is in its windings among the open wolds. It would be vastly interesting to analyse what it is that accounts for these differences, but that would be to let Cotswold steal the prime interest of this book right away from the Thames. Let it suffice to conclude this imaginary tracing of the elusive watershed by noting its far limits that really are the beginnings of the Thames.

It would find the dividing height falling away sadly from the 900-ft. ridge of Snowshill and Stanway, and the 650-ft. saddle between Charlton Abbots and Brockhampton, whence Coln nearly flows away into the Severn by the beggarly 475-ft. " summit " that the Gloucester highway sweeps over so disdainfully. It would rise again in true Cotswold style past " St. Paul's Epistle "—a lone clump of

THE SEVEN SPRINGS, SOURCE OF THE CHURN.

fir trees—only to swoop down Chatcombe Pitch to the road-junction where the Cirencester–Cheltenham road, that has faithfully followed all the windings of the Churn thus far, now finds the little river's very beginning at its " Seven Springs ".

This source of the Churn is claimed to be the farthest from the ocean of all Thames water. Whether this can be disputed or not, the " Seven Springs " rise notably high— close on the 700-ft. level, and perilously near, from the point of view of Thames territory, to taking the wrong turning, for only across the roadway, where it forks into four at this " col " of the ridge-top, the drop begins that leads swiftly down to Cheltenham and the West.

Certainly the " Seven Springs " can claim a vast superiority in height over the other " Thames Head ", which forms a pool in a flat meadow by the roadway south-westward out of Cirencester. Less than 400 feet is the height above sea-level of this beginning of the Thames. Yet, from this very source, it is the true and authentic Thames. It begins, not as a hill-brook, but winding level among meadows that form pasture right to its bank, as they do away down-river as far as there is any country on the Thames—below Shillingford Bridge, or on Cock Marsh opposite Bourne End, or even down between Boveney and Windsor.

Also, it is noticeable, this River Thames takes possession of its territory as it flows and grows; it imprints its own character, steady-going and unhurried, on this peaceful stretch of country, where there is little of note to describe, but where the country and the river make a picture of quiet. A country of wide open stretches, with few woods and only sparse trees and hedges, this real Upper Thames looks away to Cotswolds, to Berkshire Downs and to the western counties, but it belongs to none but itself. It receives Churn and Coln and Leach as they come to it; but Cricklade and Lechlade, where they join it, are Thames towns. So is Fairford, where the noble church, so well-known, with its stories in stained-glass windows, is always worth a pilgrim-age, as also is Ampney Crucis, where the carvings of the tiny church and the beautiful churchyard cross are a delight to find because they are so unknown.

From the admission, grudgingly made just now, that there is little of note to describe in these early wanderings of the Thames, it might be questioned whether this Berk-shire–Wiltshire–Gloucestershire hinterland is worth ex-ploring. One may agree that it is no place for a walking-tour; the lanes wind hither and thither, and away from them, the going is heavy and ditch-beset; heights sufficient to give any view are rare, and even the towpath is of uncertain continuity. Yet, to know the Thames as a whole, and not just as a full-grown river that appears for one's enjoyment at Pangbourne, at Henley, or at Boulter's Lock, one needs at least to traverse this remote land of little brooks and wide stretches of pastoral land.

It can be done in many ways. Some may fancy a special pilgrimage to William Morris's Kelmscott, seeing that he chose his work-place for its utter seclusion and its contrast from London. The pilgrimage might well be made as a progression from the great to the small—from the great city of Oxford, through the moderate-sized country town of Witney and the smaller yet busy townlet of Bampton to the strung-out village of Clanfield and the hamlet of Radcot (though that itself is a digression and liable to lead to other such) until, past the few dwellings along the approach

THAMES HEAD, NEAR CIRENCESTER.

RADCOT BRIDGE, DATING FROM THE EARLY THIRTEENTH CENTURY.

roads, one finds the only thing that matters in Kelmscott—the manor-house that was to be the power-house for regenerating English arts and crafts.

The manor-house is charming—more than charming—for it is grand in its finished stone-work and its fine proportions, from whatever point one views it. Yet it is hardly correct to call it the only thing that matters in Kelmscott; for the church, with William Morris's grave in the churchyard, is perfectly fitting. So is the Morris memorial hall; and the paths to the river enable one to link Thames with country and enjoy the atmosphere of calm and quiet that still pervades Kelmscott.

Some communities of a very different type might be visited by a variation of the route from Witney. Minster Lovell, down by the Windrush below the great Gloucester highway, is a Mecca for the lover of picturesque ruins; along the highway all types of "temporary" service erections cover several square miles; and down a left turn towards Brize Norton the almost unique experiment of Charterville Allotments forms an attempt at country settlement which is the reverse of dormitory ribbon-development.

This, however, provides an instance of how easily one finds other interests, even when setting out with one avowed object. Another explorer may be content to roam at large and take as they come whatever villages may lie in his track : some writers have urged that every English village is worth a visit for some feature that is distinctively its own. This philosophy might justify a stop to scrutinize Broughton Poggs, though to the passing eye it presents no distinctive architecture in its pig-sties, and little that is more prepossessing than its name. Thus, while not ruling out the possibility, nay, the inevitability, of discovering charm and interest in many rural corners, it may be wise to make each tour a "tour with an object".

One such might include, in reasonable mileage, quite a number of the ancient Thames bridges. Whether or not one penetrates so far upstream as Thames Head road-bridge by Cirencester, or the footbridge at Inglesham round-house, these bridges are a noble company. The many stout arches at Wallingford and at Abingdon make sure of keeping clear of flooded marshes; Henley and Shillingford manage with fewer, through choosing higher and harder banks that confine the stream; all are noteworthy in preserving ancient river-crossings, and all are worth visiting for the different views of the reaches above and below. The chances they give of enjoying the varying aspects of Thames make it advisable to allow ample time for a tour conducted on these lines; it has been well said that bridges are not things to go over, so much as things to stand on and look over; but Thames bridges fulfil both functions admirably.

Two of the oldest and most historically interesting are especially deserving of a stop, both for themselves and for the typical bits of Thames on which they look up and down. Radcot Bridge, a few miles east of Kelmscott where the road runs south to Faringdon, was the scene of the fateful skirmish of Richard II's time, familiar in *Richard of Bordeaux*. New Bridge, still farther down river where a southward road from Witney crosses to reach Abingdon or Wantage, is new only relatively; Radcot is thought to have been there already when this bridge was built about 1250.

The Fairford–Faringdon road uses yet another ancient crossing at St. John's Bridge below Lechlade. This dates from 1229, though records tell of rebuilding in the fourteenth century, and the present bridge was erected in 1820.

It is noticeable how frequently Faringdon crops up as the destination of these cross-country roads; Faringdon was the metropolis of the Vale of White Horse in *Tom Brown's Schooldays*, and it is still a fine old town to include in any itinerary. So, in a smaller way, is Highworth, farther west, on another hillock—the centre of a distinct section of rural Berkshire.

These southward roads, over the Thames and across the vale, all strike at one point or another, the venerable road east and west below the Berkshire Downs. Some fall in and follow its sinuous up-and-down course, like the one from Lechlade that crosses the Thames by St. John's Bridge and runs by Faringdon to Wantage, thereby visiting the truest towns and the most typical country of the Vale of White Horse. Others strike boldly up over the Down wherever they can find the least precipitous route, like the

THE BRIDGE AT
CLIFTON HAMPDEN,
NOW FREE OF TOLL.

THE VILLAGE OF
CLIFTON HAMPDEN,
BELOW ABINGDON.

Abingdon–Newbury road, or the road from Oxford that
soars up the open hillside behind Wantage, sinks gradually
down between deepening green banks to cross the Lambourn
valley, and fares on over another ridge to the woods of the
Kennet down Hungerford way.   One road seems to dis-
regard the old road, even though it crosses it, but that is
only because it is a Roman road, disregarding everything
except its own destination.   It has come almost dead
straight from Gloucester over Birdlip Hill to Cirencester;
there it gathers itself for another mighty step on its way to
Silchester.   Thames throws it out of its stride just a little
where it has to choose a crossing by Cricklade (at present,
that is: the Romans crossed lower down, not far off their
direct line).   Thereafter it marches straight as possible
over the Vale and the intervening hillocks; its own village
of Stratton St. Margaret huddles close by it as it leaves
Swindon disdainfully away to the west and drives straight
at the hillside and up to the Totterdown Inn, where even

THE VILLAGE CROSS AT EAST HAGBOURNE.

FARINGDON FOLLY, A LANDMARK OF THE VALE OF WHITE HORSE.

a Roman road has to pause to take notice of the ridge-way on the crest. It is interesting, too, in passing, to notice a characteristic liberty which the Wiltshire cottager takes with this august highway; a mile or so from the foot of the down, a cottage-gardener took advantage of the generous width between hedges to plant a vegetable patch bordering on the macadam. In course of years the roadway, having plenty of room on the other side as well, began to swing away from the cultivation, until the emboldened gardener actually grew a little secondary hedge around the verge of his plot, thus implanting on the arrow-like itinerary of the legions that abomination to the Roman—a curve away from the direct line.

Only very minor modifications, however, have touched the course of these immemorial ways across both river and hills. By such routes as these, one can truly see the variety of scene that makes up the Thames country, and appreciate the common and complementary interests that bind the parts into the whole.

## CHAPTER SEVEN

# THE BERKSHIRE SIDE

IT might be argued that the Kennet, as the original progenitor of the Thames, might fairly claim more than part of a belated chapter.

Kennet country, however, has not a great deal of variety. One sound reason for this—geology again—is that for centuries the Kennet was quietly laying down feet upon feet of the alluvium that grows its present-day crops, while the upstart Goring stream, the cuckoo in the nest that has now grown so overmastering, was carving out its gorge through the chalk.

Viewed in this light, the Kennet valley claims the respect due to age. From the centre of its long, straight trough, where river and canal, railway and Bath road, all follow the line of least resistance, the fields spread north and south, to rise gradually and naturally to the little hills that fringe the higher chalkier hills beyond. It seems a country where the rhythmic swing of the farmer's year recurs without end —hardly the country to bring any thrills of exciting discovery.

Yet suppose that a cyclist, attracted by such names as Sulhampstead Bannister and Sulhampstead Abbots, accepts the assistance of the Great Western Railway, as suggested earlier, as far as Theale.

Road and railway sweep on westward, and the little hills where those villages are to be found seem far away southward over the levels. Kennet in all its branches seems a less leisurely stream here than one would expect in such flat country; the southward road crosses quite a maze of waters hurrying away towards the Thames. Rising gently past copses of oak and ash, with chestnut and holly intermingled, the lane catches a view far ahead of the Hampshire border hills, dips again, and climbs between high banks to a tiny triangle of green.

Here stands the little church of Sulhampstead Abbots, flint-built with a tiled and boarded steeple-gable; one timbered-and-thatched house stands close by, another appears round the corner of the lane, and fields beyond roll away towards the neighbour church of Sulhampstead Bannister with its farm buildings alongside.

Bearing westward along the right-hand lane—a lane with lovely open woodland over a low wall, the wall itself thick with moss and ferns—there appears yet another church—the graceful spire of Ufton Nervet. The lane straightens out and heads for a right-and-left turn, where a signpost stands white against the darkness of fir woods, darkness that is set off by the green or brown, according to season, of the oaks that line the low banks of the road. This is a country of low banks that allow of distant views wherever a dip of the rolling countryside falls away on either hand—a country, too, of magnificent oak trees, relics of the great oak forest that formerly covered most of Berkshire. The colours of the leaves on a bright autumn day make a ride among these lanes a memory to carry through the winter.

From this little upland, it is possible to run down southward to Silchester, where a great part of the wall, four feet thick and eight feet high, still stands as it stood encircling the Roman city, and where the surname " Cæsar " appears on a comparatively modern tombstone by the little steepled church inside the wall. Or, south-easterly, by the parklands and the orderly village of Stratfield Mortimer, one may touch upon the valley of the Loddon, which curves round towards Reading from the commons of north Hampshire—different type of country altogether.

More likely, however, the westward urge may lead still along the lanes that look southward across five miles of wooded vale to the high clear humps of the Hampshire Downs. At any point along this little intermediate ridge, one can choose a by-way dipping down to whatever station suits for the return journey by rail. A mile downhill and a mile or two of level brings one to Aldermaston, or Midgham, or Thatcham, or—to round off a tour of fifteen, twenty, thirty miles, whichever one likes to make it—to Newbury itself.

Newbury, the metropolis of the Kennet valley, is an excellent natural centre for exploring by any method both the rural villages that surround it or the high open downs north, north-west, and south. Especially is this true of the Hampshire hill-tops to the south, wonderfully rich both in prehistoric remains and in sudden, arresting view-points. This, however, is country rather remote from the Thames, both in distance and in character. So, too, is the upper Kennet valley a few miles beyond Newbury. The hills, crowding closer on all sides, show the clean bare outlines of the Wiltshire chalk country; and Silbury Hill and the Marlborough Downs, to say nothing of Savernake Forest or the Vale of Pewsey, are Wessex rather than Thames.

There is one off-shoot from the Kennet that seems to link vale with hills. The Lambourn valley, which penetrates into the down north-westward, broadens out to help make Newbury the strategic point it is, where half a dozen natural routes converge.

The Lambourn valley is emphatically a valley to explore upwards, past Boxford and Welford, Shelford and Garston —all compact and comfortable-looking little communities, sheltering in the valley but looking up to the bare though

THE FAMOUS
OLD CLOTH
HALL AT
NEWBURY.

THE GIBBET ON
INKPEN BEACON,
ON THE HAMPSHIRE
BORDER SOUTH-WEST
OF NEWBURY.

WATER-MILL AT DENFORD, NEAR HUNGERFORD.

not unkindly downs around them, and existing partly by virtue of sheep, but mainly by the horse. Beyond Lambourn itself roads are few, but tracks abound, and they all alike lead ultimately to the great chalk ridge-top of White Horse Hill.

This glorious open hill-top of the Berkshire Downs is Wessex unquestionably, but it also belongs to the Thames. Thames Valley without White Horse Down can hardly be imagined, so inevitably does it figure in every view southward from beyond the river; and the prospect over all the Upper Thames from Liddington, from Uffington, or from Segsbury Camp, from Wayland's Smithy or from any other point along the Ridge Way, is one which, knowing not, one knows not the Thames.

The Vale of White Horse belongs to the Thames, too, though it belongs to itself as well, and has as distinct characteristics as any section of the whole Thames Valley. One can survey the Vale from the ridge-top along the pre-historic turf track—one of the earliest travel-ways of this country—or explore it along the hill-foot, where an almost equally ancient roadway winds as near the level as it can find firm going for its age-long traffic. If it is possible to trace both routes, so much the better, for the villages that are strung along the base of the downs, some tucked away in gullies, some spread out along the verge of the levels, are all worth a digression.

Typical of them is West Challow, where a lane diverging from the hill-foot road leads to the tiny fourteenth-century church with its beautifully carved porch and chancel screen, and, in its turret, one of the oldest bells in England, bearing the legend, " Paul Potter me fist, 1282 ".

This hill-foot road winds close under the rise of the down. It passes the " Blowing Stone " of *Tom Brown's Schooldays* ; it twists suddenly in and out of a sharp hollow in the green rampart that towers above, and there on the very crest is the Great White Horse itself. It passes signpost after signpost that says " Sparsholt ", until one thinks " Spar's holt—Sparrow's Holt—the holt of the Sparrow Hawk—could this have been the country where, of old, Tennyson's Prince Geraint found and fought the Sparrow Hawk Knight? " Anything recorded of ancient days is possible in this Wessex countryside, whether of King Arthur's Knights or of King Alfred and his struggles with the Danes; for this is the country of the beginnings of English history, and in the market square of Wantage, his own home town, stands the statue of King Alfred himself.

It would be easy to let the magic and legend, and the history and interest of the White Horse country steal the time and attention one wants to devote to the many-sidedness of the Thames. For another aspect of the complete picture, one may note, before passing down-river, a small and easily overlooked corner where one of the minor tributaries pursues its own quiet course.

The little River Pang is hardly observable at all where

THE LAMBOURN VALLEY RISING TO THE DOWNS.

it joins the Thames, even though its name-town of Pang-bourne takes possession so thoroughly and so fittingly of its particular reach. The confluence is between the weir and the bridge; the little stream is so covered in by roads and railway, and the dash of the weir so screens the inflow, that one has to search carefully—disregarding the scenic features that are so exceptionally interesting just here. This is the point, as one sees looking across weir and islets, where the hills on both sides stand in so close as to give hardly any room for country at all. So it appears up-stream; but look downward to the broadening valley, or, better still, cross the Pangbourne–Whitchurch toll-bridge (only one penny return, and the custodian so worthily upholds that standard of cheerfulness mentioned in Chapter Six as to rob the extortion of all sting). Turn right where the beechwoods rising close ahead give warning of Chiltern territory, and in only a few hundred yards one seems to have strayed into a wide, poplar-studded expanse with little sign of town or railway, hills or river, where meadows extend to the misty limits of vision.

This unobtrusiveness of the Pang extends to its begin-nings as well as to its end. Its valley is in some ways a miniature of the Kennet, yet different.

Suppose that a tourist, instead of railway, chooses the Bath road, and has had enough of it by the time Aldermaston looms ahead. A turn to the right leads up a wooded hill-side to Beenham; or better still, an earlier by-way climbs a steeper hill-side to Beenham Stocks. It rises past oak and ash thickets; it passes cottages among orchards which in sound Thames Valley fashion clothe the southward-facing slope—though well away from the ash trees, for ash is not a good neighbour to fruit. This is one of those steepening roads which lead on by promising to show something worth seeing at the top.

THE FLY, PAINTED ON
A WINDOW IN
BUCKLEBURY CHURCH.

EARLY CARVING IN
INGLESHAM CHURCH.

THE STATUE OF KING
ALFRED, IN WANTAGE
WHERE HE WAS BORN
IN 849.

So, in a mild Thames Valley sort of way, it does. Immediately one gains the crest of this quite minor ridge, where the Stocks Inn marks the site where " they say " the village stocks used to be set up, the higher hills away northward begin to appear; but there are several dips and rises worth exploring before they will be in full and close view.

Beenham church, flint built with a big square brick tower, lies down a lane with several footpaths radiating from its end. The lane rises to a knoll with a fine view east and west along the valley, with the Hampshire ridges away to the south. Beenham village has a number of intriguing twisty by-ways to thread before the westward route dips down across a secondary valley where the Bourne, a sub-tributary of the Pang, makes its own way downhill—a mere field-side trickle but preserving its independence almost down to the Thames.

Beyond a roadside farm, where a huge thatched barn makes its broad roof visible far away, the lane gives signs of approaching open country, for footpaths branch off into scrub, and the hedges fall back to curve into the noble length of Bucklebury Avenue. A double line of magnificent oaks can be seen stretching far ahead; hedges beyond the wide grassy verges show farm roofs above the slopes that fall away right and left, and the avenue leads on to the high breezy expanse of Bucklebury Common.

Three miles of common, a mile wide, were within a few months turned into a mammoth dump, station, and distributing centre for war-time transport. How many years it will take, after the last hut and direction-post have been cleared away, for the Common to become really common again, can only be guessed. The dead-straight road along its centre will always command a view worthy of its elevation; but to enjoy the woodland wildness of this secluded ridge, one must try the side-lanes that curl down on either hand.

H

One such turns sharp right for Bucklebury village from a road-fork half-way along the summit-road. Following it down between scrub-coppice and steeply-sloping fields, with here and there the grandest of oak trees, one wonders what manner of village Bucklebury can be, to stand possessed of such an imposing Common. Presently it appears, scattered cottages in their gay gardens, and a group of solid dwellings around the church. Bucklebury seems quite dominated by the church, with its generous-bodied nave, window gables in the tiled roof, and broad, square tower that holds the eye as the road curves round to the churchyard entrance.

The tower continues to hold the interest as one walks close under it to look up at the truly grotesque gargoyles round the coping. It is angled with the stout " long and short work " that sets the antiquary looking for other Norman details; and, sure enough, they are there. The

BLEWBURY UNDER THE BERKSHIRE DOWNS, NEAR WALLINGFORD.

south porch is dated outside—a mere 1603; but within it, the main doorway shows a fine Norman arch with chevron moulding surmounted by distinctive carving. Inside, the old box-pews are plainly and simply fashioned, with some, older still, of rough-hewn timber slab. Inside and out, Bucklebury church has a quiet dignity that is enhanced by its setting among the riverside meadows, with the long valley stretching westward between its enclosing banks of hill.

The footpath finder will rejoice to see the pair of swing-gates northward from the church. A path leads thence to a little stone bridge over the Pang; the bridge gives the path a straight line which the road curves into—sure sign of an ancient way—and, half a mile on, the road forks right

and left.   The path keeps on, though, into a wood, thick
with rank and rampant undergrowth, straight for a stile
that finds fields again ahead of it, stretching away to—
whatever point among the wooded hills beyond that the
walker may choose to find.

Paths in plenty lead from Bucklebury up to the Common,
too, and every one finds a different woodland way to the
crest.   For the roadfarer, also, there is ample choice among
the half-dozen lanes that converge on Bucklebury.

From the road-fork just mentioned—leaving the footpath to allure its own devotees—the left-hand way curves
up between wooded banks to a broad expanse of farm land.
It passes a wayside farm with a noble array of barn-roofs
and thatched ricks, en route to Frilsham and Hampstead
Norris, where it climbs through thin, high woodland out to
the open downs beyond Compton.   To taste the downland,
one might follow it on to East Ilsley (of sheep-fair fame)
and over the shoulder of the main Berkshire Downs to those
hill-foot villages that form such a fascinating chain from
Wantage down towards Wallingford.

That means deserting the Pang, however, almost as soon
as it is found.   Turning right after leaving Bucklebury, a
road runs parallel with the river—parallel also with paths
that try to follow the river's bank but find marsh and ditch
too insistent here and there.   A couple of miles on,
Stanford Dingley spreads out, between road and river, its
assemblage of cottages and farm buildings.   The little
tile-roofed church, with its timbered steeple, stands up from
the road inside the lych-gate; and below it, diverging from
the road but keeping its own straight line, a path leads to a
footbridge, presumably at the point where, in good Berkshire talk, the Stawan-ford first provided a crossing.
(Place-name etymology is notoriously full of pitfalls, but
this one is at least more credible than many.)

THE RIVER PANG,
NEAR BUCKLEBURY:
SOMETIMES DRY,
SOMETIMES FULL.

*Left :* WATER-MILL
ON THE PANG AT
STANFORD
DINGLEY.

BRADFIELD COLLEGE, IN THE VALLEY OF THE PANG.

The Pang valley has the same characteristic as the Kennet —a long, shallow trough, level by the stream and rising evenly to the wooded side-hills—the handiwork of a well-behaved little river. Down by Bradfield—a more considerable village, with the college buildings making a handsome group up the slope—the woods come closer, and a left turn soon leads up into thick oak and larch, with beech showing all its delicate shades at any season. Dipping steeply to a fork, this road bears up again to height enough for a look back over tree-tops all round, with paths striking away along the crest, where the road levels out to run by rough fields and patches of broom into Upper Basildon.

Whether Upper Basildon is worth a visit for its own sake or not, it provides many ways for penetrating farther into the uplands by Ashampstead or Aldworth, or for returning

to the Thames. One of the choicest of the latter is the
direct run down to Pangbourne; the valley towards Goring
and beyond opens up leftwards, but ahead the broad butt-
end of the Chiltern ridge stands up close, though it is the
other side of the river; and all too soon the road is dropping
into the main road along which Pangbourne makes the most
of its charming river-frontage.

Across the main road, however, one again finds the little
Pang stream, making its way as unobtrusively as ever into
Father Thames. Its valley is a notable instance of how
much beauty is to be found in any corner of the Thames
country by the discerning explorer.

## CHAPTER EIGHT

## DOWN THE THAMES ITSELF

THERE was mention earlier of the little hills in the middle Thames Valley that drive the river to such pronounced looping and curving, and at the same time provide such unexpected view-points.

One such patch of hilly country, typical yet unique, is responsible for the river's decided departure from a straight line between Reading and Windsor. The London road out of Reading keeps straighter by leaving these hills on its left, with the river winding northward past Henley, easterly by Marlow, and then south to beyond Maidenhead. Fortunately the road back to London is rich in possible digressions, and almost any turn left beyond Reading's eastern suburbs will find a choice country route to the river again.

Among the well-known, and deservedly popular parts of the Thames, the ten-mile stretch from Reading down to Henley stands high, mainly by virtue of its little riverside towns. Sonning, Wargrave, and Shiplake all have character of their own, and all have their special devotees.

Sonning village is well-known but ever charming none the less. Even buses digress from the Bath road to thread their way round sharp corners and between high walls, where clematis and wistaria train over plaster and black beams, and curious angles and gables project in a most pleasing assembly of gardens—well-kept and full of colour. Farther on, at Knowle Hill, another turn left penetrates at once a part where the clematis is the wild

variety—the familiar and rampant Old Man's Beard. Take
the lane for Warren Row where the little church of Knowle
Hill—flint and brick, with a tiny sharp spire—stands back
among its screen of trees, and immediately the Bath road
seems far away. Thick hedges of thorn and oak saplings
stand well back across the grassy verges; the lane rounds
a bend past a grand group of farm buildings with lichened
red-brown roofing-tiles, and over the hedge there stand
up massive, square-built chimneys that catch the eye at
once.

They bring one to a stop inevitably, facing the Red
House Inn. It stands invitingly back—solid brick with
timber out-buildings, and the interior is exactly fitting too.
Behind it the fields roll away to a dip and rise, with fir
woods on the far slope, and through the gap that drops
Thameswards the hills on the north bank rise away up to the
distant sky-line—a delightful prospect.

Close by the bend of the lane, a track leads gently downwards, strikes the Hurley–Henley road just by the " Black
Boy ", and continues on to the ferry where the steep bluffs
of Medmenham stand high on the other side.

Or, from the tiny patch of green facing the " Red House ",
where pheasants wander at large and a few tiled roofs show
among apple trees, tracks and paths lead up to Bowsey Hill.
There, from the wood-fringe, with Wargrave Marsh lying
far below, one can look up the river-valley with nothing to
interrupt the view for miles beyond Reading.

Another way is to follow the road on through Warren
Row, and Cockpole Green, past the " Old House at Home ",
past the " Four Horseshoes ", hanging in their handsome
wrought-iron sign, and still farther—beyond a right turn
from the main road towards Aston Ferry—the " Five
Horseshoes ". Then another turn right leads away down
to Remenham; but before descending so far a lovely wood

SOME OF THE MANY ARCHES OF SONNING BRIDGE.

of beech and spruce, oak and ash and chestnut, with here and there a huge old wild cherry, covers the slope of the hill-side. Paths lead here and there, some to the steep bank overlooking the Henley road in a deep cutting, some to the wood-edge looking down at Phyllis Court and Remenham; or the timber-tracks can be followed until sometimes, here within a mile of Henley Regatta Reach, one finds a couple of woodmen plying axe and saw in the depths of this still, secluded woodland. They show a wonderful art in " falling " the tall slim spruce among the ranks of beech that are awaiting the thinning to grow into massive trees themselves. They cast an eye around to decide the line where the tree must drop. They " put in the fall " : that is to say, they chop a notch on the side where they want it to fall clear of other trees. Then the cross-cut sings its song for perhaps ten minutes with no other sound, until there comes a crack, and a gentle crash if there can be such a thing; with an eight-ft. rod they measure off 40 feet; the axe swings—just right, left, and one, two, three—the head of the tree is severed and a potential telegraph-pole waits to be dragged away.

From these rural solitudes, a variety of ways can lead back towards London. One is the nearly-riverside road over Henley Bridge and round the big Hambleden bend, into Buckinghamshire; another on the southern bank swoops down towards river-level and keeps along the foot of the wooded slope, past the turn for Hurley, and into Marlow by Bisham. Even the semi-main roads hereabouts discover some beautiful stretches of woodland. The one that turns left off the Bath road by Littlewick Green for Burchetts Green swings downhill under scattered oaks that reach their great branches clear across the road. Then, round a bend where one solitary oak stands out and makes the road sweep round it, the oak trees end, and the road

ROAD-BRIDGE AND FOOT-BRIDGE AT SONNING.

becomes an avenue of beech, lovely in colouring at all times, but especially when the autumn sun after an early frost brings out the golden-brown of the leaves. Down towards Temple, the flat river-meadows spread out level, with farms and rick-yards just at the foot of the rising ground; the road looks out over mile after mile of valley through fine, big, spaced-out beeches on the lower side, while sharply up to the right the woods climb thick and high. Those hill-slope woods continue on, to join with Quarry Woods facing Marlow. The road slants down to pass by Bisham, where groups of mellow-brick cottages, with dormer-windows in their tiled roofs, stand beautifully by the church.

It is not strictly necessary to follow the main road through Marlow if one chooses to vary the route. Before crossing Marlow Bridge, a minor road, twisting but lovely, turns right to climb through Quarry Woods, which have been admired from below several times in the course of the ramblings mentioned earlier, and can now be enjoyed close at hand, before dropping into the maze of ups and downs, steps and lanes and wooded dells that make up the picturesqueness of Cookham Dean. This must not, however, be taken as an injunction to avoid Marlow. Of all the charming little towns up and down the river, Marlow can perhaps be singled out as specially belonging to the Thames. It enjoys its river; without the river it would hardly be Marlow; and conversely, if one is to paint a true picture of the Thames as a whole, Marlow must not be left out.

Some travellers coming down-stream say that Marlow is the last of the real river towns. Like Abingdon and Wallingford and Henley, it has a personality distinctively its own; and each one of those four is unquestionably both a river town and a country town; each forms a link between the river and the neighbouring country. Marlow's special stretch of country lies mostly down-river, where the valley broadens out to let farms spread their fields wide and level. Higher up, the woods and private estates of Medmenham and Hurley, Temple and Bisham, fill most of the low ground and the riverside heights as well. In all the length of the Thames, this is one section where " river-country " is most noticeably narrowed down, for the Chilterns run close down from the north, and Maidenhead Thicket to the south hints at the proximity of London.

Below Marlow, however, the hills run back from the northern bank, and leave a feeling of spaciousness more than proportionate to the couple of miles of level farm-lands that border the stream. Here, the river is the genuine country Thames again. Cattle browse down to the very banks, wade in the shallows, and wander from the towpath to the Marlow railway that has no gradient whatever in its three-mile length. Real farming country is this

THE BULL INN, SONNING VILLAGE.

too, where the crops tell the tale of deep rich soil, and the massive barns and corn-ricks make fine specimens of rural architecture.

Hereabouts, also, the walker comes into his own again. Barely a mile out of Marlow, along the east-bound road, a by-road bears sharply left. It curves gently uphill past chalk-pits and banks of flowering weeds—lovely in colour for all that—towards Burroughs Grove, a hamlet where a real road climbing a real hill can be seen ahead. Neither need be heeded, however, for a footpath breaks off to the right, dips along the field-sides, and swings up again to the corner of a wood just high enough on the shoulder of a rise to command the valley below. From here, a footpath slants half-right across a sloping field. It may, however, be found either heavy going after wet weather, or deep in growing corn, and to avoid both mud and crops an alternative way leads into the wood.

A lovely, shady wood is this, with willow-herb and wild strawberry filling the gaps between the trees. A timber-hauling track winds left and right, finally slithering down to a by-road that curves between cornfields and pasture towards the Marlow road again. Thence, either footpath over the next brow, or field-track across the level, will be found to lead infallibly to Little Marlow.

This is a village that hides away off the road, where all turnings are marked " No Through Road "; but it is worth going down one of them and back another to see the truly pretty cottages and well-kept gardens of Little Marlow.

Cyclists who take that same turn off the Marlow main road may choose to make a wider detour from Burroughs Grove. The highroad uphill takes only a mile to climb high enough to command the whole of this reach of river and the curvings of the Thames both up-stream and down. This is the spot from which to see the little town of Marlow, compact, busy and thriving, with its church spire standing prominently by the suspension bridge against the lovely background of Quarry Woods up the far bank. Leftwards the slope carries the eye to the broad shining reach from Marlow down to Bourne End. There the river, making its great bend towards the south, meets the hills close to, loops round the base of Hedsor parish (this scattered parish may be investigated more closely before leaving this hill-and-valley region), and runs under Cliveden Woods towards the civilization of Boulter's Lock and Maidenhead.

Between there and here, however, lies a seclusion of country that could never be mistaken for any other district than Thames. The map shows names such as Ragman's Castle, Oldhouse Farm, and Handycross; and at that last-named point, where the Chiltern look begins to creep into

HENLEY IN
REGATTA WEEK.

HENLEY BRIDGE
AND CHURCH,
AND THE RIVER
UP-STREAM.

the distance, a lane turns right to drop down Thamesward once more.

It swings down between gently curving banks into a lovely dell where the couple of farms of Winchbottom lie surrounded by wood-edged fields—a little haven of quietness where the breeze from the river-valley just brushes the tree tops. The lane curves right, falling gently still, and glides down a side-valley filled on both sides with tall, slim beech trees, well spaced out to let the sun light up the depths where moss and violets, or willow-herb and wild rose, cover every stump and stone. The easy run-down of the road swings left and right round successive swelling rises of green hill-side that broaden out imperceptibly to the level fields along the hill-foot, and there among elm trees the brown roofs of Little Marlow cluster round the grey church tower, with the Thames again only a mile away across the fields.

Still another by-road turns left off that eastbound road along this straight level stretch of valley. A signpost points to " Sheepridge ", and a barer winding road climbs up again to the scattered cottages and cherry orchards of Heath End. It bears right, round the head of a dip that gives a beautiful view back towards Marlow, and, keeping right all the time, through as many cherry trees to the acre as one will see in a day's run, another lane comes clear of the woods. It invites a pause above a steepish drop, at a gap just right for the view. Flat meadows on both sides of the river, which curves here through scattered dwellings and tree-clumps, run level right and left, with Winter Hill beyond them on the far side, steep and green. Wide round its eastward end the river makes its great bend, and from the bank there stand up those tall, swaying ranks of poplars that grow so fittingly in the landscape of the Thames.

From this outlook on the brow the lane drops down,

I

shady with elm and chestnut, to come sharply into the Marlow–Bourne End road at the hamlet of Well End.

It is possible to look out so carefully at this blind corner, as to overlook the cottage that forms its actual angle. Its fine stout timber framing stands well after the wear of centuries; and others like it make up a pleasing length of street. Even though it means turning back Marlow-wards (only for a quarter-mile) there is far more attraction this way than left towards Bourne End. The " Black Lion " stands back on one side, and the " Old Forge " on the other with a large clock overhanging its front bearing the welcome legend " It's always time for tea "—and a pleasant oak-timbered interior adds to the attraction.

The buildings along Well End street harmonize very pleasingly, ending with a fine stone-built farmhouse looking riverwards across its meadows. Opposite, there stands the lovely Old Malt House, a long and solid Queen Anne house in mellow brick and tile, with cornices and dormer-

REMENHAM CHURCH, CLOSE BY THE REGATTA COURSE.

windows, vines and wistaria, showing above its lichened wall.

A few yards farther westward, a signpost points left to " Spade Oak Ferry ", with the warning " No Through Road ". It is so for cars, but any cyclists who are determined digressors need not boggle at the few trifling obstacles between here and the river bank.

The lane winds gently downhill (for the road-junction stands on a rise of just those few feet that give a fresh view up-valley) past timbered-and-thatched cottages here and there, bowered in fruit trees, to a bend facing the great weathered barns and farmhouse of Spade Oak Farm. This lane has been an ancient way from the hills to the ferry for many generations, and many generations have obviously occupied Spade Oak Farm, standing there solid and purposeful, a type of that country life that follows its course season by season as the Thames follows its course close by.

A footpath with stile and swing-gate strikes away half-left towards the riverside bungalows and house-boats; to the right, a gated level-crossing over the single-track Marlow line leads into the broad open pasture that is bounded by the river's edge; and here is Spade Oak Ferry— a river crossing for many years, though now less frequently used, since all the barges are power-drawn. A tug with a couple of lighters will occasionally come chugging up or down; but otherwise all the river traffic is for pleasure, and craft of every variety make good use of this reach. It is the favoured water of the Upper Thames Sailing Club, whose club-house and foreshore a few yards down are lined with " Internationals " and " Twelves " that find this open two miles of river the best sailing reach of all the Thames.

A part of the river well worth visiting is this breezy bank by Spade Oak. It will be reached without fail by those walkers whose wanderings have brought them by

THE TITHE BARN
AND DOVE-COTE
AT HURLEY
AND (below)
SOME OF THE
REMAINING
BUILDINGS OF
ST. MARY'S PRIORY.

field-path and lane as far as the seclusion of Little Marlow. From the lych-gate of the church, a stony by-road winds round farm buildings into open field, and there, looking back, one sees the perfect picture of the village church above the red-brown roofs, with majestic elm and chestnut ringing it round.

A narrow lane, not much more than a rutted track between low hedges of briar, hazel, and oak, heads away towards the river, with every gap showing the high bank of woods away on the Berkshire side. This track also crosses the Marlow railway into open meadow that looks across at the high steep side of Winter Hill rising beyond the opposite bank.

A mile of towpath follows the reedy verge of the river down to Spade Oak. A path then continues down past bungalows and boat-houses and all manner of moored craft; but the official towpath crosses here, and walkers who hanker for the heights after these water-level strollings may well do the same.

A wide expanse of field spreads away behind the ferry-house, and one finds that to walk to Winter Hill, that seemed to rise so steep and near, entails half a mile of skirting boggy patches and pools fringed with flag and bulrush. A pleasant half-mile it is, though, discovering en route a tiny hidden farmhouse with one huge barn whose majestic sweep of roof, broken by a grand entrance-bay, covers both barn and cart-shed with one great slope of lichened tiles. Just beyond, the hill begins its sudden rise, a surprisingly steep promontory of chalk that drives the Thames into a decided change of course. Paths have to slant up the face as best they can. One way is to keep well to the right, rising gradually to the open top where a grand view of the valley, up, down, and across to the Chilterns, can be enjoyed at leisure before turning down the reverse

MARLOW CHURCH
SEEN THROUGH
THE ARCH OF THE
SUSPENSION BRIDGE.

THE RIVER AND
TOW-PATH ABOVE
MARLOW BRIDGE.

slope into the dells and lanes and winding paths of Cookham Dean.

A steeper path climbs the hill more directly, and bears left towards the top among gorse and brambles and clumps of holly—a fine breezy walk with the beginnings of cultivation on the right and the hill-face dropping steeply to the left. Ahead across the river, which has here swung southward under Cliveden Woods, the facing hill of Hedsor shows some curious towers among its tree-tops, and also a tiny church which may be visited anon by those who wish. The towpath, reached by a track from the hill-foot, can be followed down-stream to Cookham Bridge, now (1947) one of the bridges freed from toll.

Instead of taking that direction, however, an alternative is to cross by the Bourne End Ferry and thence take the Hedsor Road, for just hereabouts lies an area of unusual interest in the life history of the Thames country.

In the days when river traffic brought the main supply of heavy goods to and from the valley towns, the barges bringing up coal and carrying down corn had their regular routine and their recognized depots. One such loading point was at Hedsor Wharf, where one branch of the stream, now a private backwater, gave navigable depth close under Hedsor Hill on the outside of that great bend of the river noticed before. Every waterman knows that the stronger scour of the current on the outside of a bend keeps the channel deep and clear.

Hedsor Wharf then—for in that wide Spade Oak Reach before the days of the Thames Conservancy's efficient locking and regulating, the variations of the channel might seriously impede navigation farther up—became to a great extent the land-and-water transfer-point, the limit of navigation for certain classes of goods. Produce from the up-valley farms, from the hills round, and even through the

Chilterns from the Vale of Aylesbury, converged on this natural shipping-point.

A memory of those times can be recalled on the way to Hedsor through Upper Bourne End. The main road to Cookham curves over the little Wye stream—nearing its confluence with the Thames—past a house with wonderfully trained ivy trellissing its front. Just beyond, a secondary road forks left and rises, gently at first and then more steeply, to a junction. Between three roads meeting here, there rises a sloping triangle—field, spinney, and a few huddled cottages. Old they certainly are, and they, with the land in the triangle, go by the name of " Heaven's Lea ".

Those buildings, though now adapted for human habitation, were once, it is said, the stables for the barge-horses resting there, after their pull up-stream to Hedsor Wharf, until the barges were re-loaded for the journey down.

Such are a few of the items of interest and attraction to be discovered in one corner of the Thames Valley in this tiny parish of Hedsor, less than a square mile in total acreage, and in those few miles up-stream—once one begins to explore it. What may not further investigation bring to light in all the dozens of parishes and hundreds of square miles up and down the river?

## CHAPTER NINE

## NEARER LONDON

THE interest of the curious parish of Hedsor is by no means exhausted by those few details touched on in Chapter Eight. Some of its inhabitants who remember the custom of defining their boundaries by walking round them—known as "beating the bounds"—recall vividly the insistence of their leaders on the fact that the parish boundary passed exactly through the building of the Walnut Trees Inn on the Bourne End–Cookham road. Some modern delineators question the correctness of this contention, but the beaters of the bounds were convinced that they could do their duty properly only by passing through the cellars of the "Walnut Trees"—not without a halt en route, of course. After that they felt fortified for the further ordeal of fording the river to lay claim to an indeterminate strip of land on the Berkshire side.

Some of the ancient champions of Hedsor's boundaries aver that from that point their progression took them up the south bank as far as Bisham to perpetuate their ownership of a patch of land annexed to Bisham Abbey, some four miles up-stream.

This aggression may have been inspired by the sojourn at the "Walnut Trees". Hedsor folk actually have no need to go quite so far to claim an outlying portion of their parish, for the tithe maps of 1839 are content with one "island". Explorers who admired the village architecture of Well End had no means of knowing, but one pair of stout brick cottages just beyond the "Black Lion" appears on the

tithe maps as part of Hedsor, though standing completely
surrounded by Little Marlow.

If, however, ancient church-paths signify what they
usually do, those cottages had their footpath straight to
their church, even though it had to traverse the intervening
parish of Wooburn. From the eastern end of Well End,
where the Bourne End road swings right, a footpath, in
true footpath style, maintains a straight line. From the
junction of a rough, stony lane, it cuts between houses and
orchards, crosses another farm road—with a glorious view
up a variegated hillside, where field and wood alternate up
a long curving hollow topped by pine and beechwoods on
the sky-line—and skirts a field bordered with thick shady
bushes. Its line is jealously preserved between gardens
and across a housing estate, perfectly straight still, and,
where it strikes another road winding up between more
woods and orchards towards Flackwell Heath, there on the
far side appear again the welcome signs " Public Footpath ".

These signs point in two directions here, for one path*
forks off half-left to slant over the hill-brow towards Wooburn church; Wooburn spreads far across the valley of the
little Wye stream, which is here nearing the Thames. A
fine circle of footpath walking in that direction may be
noted later; this Hedsor path deserves to be followed
onwards first, for its line through the facing gap, beneath
the shadow of a high, thick hedge of hawthorn, will be
found to be pointing directly towards Hedsor church on the
hill-side a mile ahead. Stream, railway tracks, and mills
divert it from the straight line at Bourne End, however,
and on striking the Wooburn road one must bear left, over
a level crossing and over the Wye at Core's End—the
third of the three " Ends " one finds contiguous here.

Several steep by-roads climb the slope in front, which

* October, 1947, diverted 90 yards up to the left.

BISHAM ABBEY, UP-RIVER FROM MARLOW.

is the beginning of a high, rolling sweep of farms and field-ways. It stretches from the big estates of Dropmore and Cliveden to the remote-from-London side of Burnham Beeches, with many lanes winding among the scattered beechwoods from the Bath road by Farnham or Burnham or Hitcham towards the Beaconsfield–Oxford highway. The climb up the hill-side from Core's End is one good approach to this patch of rural Buckinghamshire, and there are several choices of route even here. Hawks Hill and Harvest Hill curve up rightwards, for a commanding sweep of view from the hill-top that surveys the river both up-stream and down. By keeping straight ahead, however—or as straight as the gentle left and right swervings of the road allow—the steep cutting of Kiln Lane winds upwards after the manner of ancient hill-ways, with a fine patch of woodland—beech, fir, and holly—bordering the right-hand bank. It is worth while scrambling up through the open margin of the wood to look away between the tree trunks at the successive curves of foothill that roll down towards Marlow. On-

MARLOW WEIR.

wards over the top, past a footpath that comes up on the left from Wooburn church in the narrowing valley northward, the river view is left behind, hidden and forgotten for the time, for a wide plateau of fields and woodlands opens up ahead.

Roads and tracks criss-cross hither and thither in a way that invites random wanderings. Oak-scrub and bracken alternate with stretches of pasture, where one senses that stillness and quietude so often found in clearings between woodlands; and the scattered farms and cottages fit their brown tiles and thatch most appropriately into the scene. At Widmoor, just beyond the sign of " The Chequers " at the top of Kiln Lane, a noble weathercock crowns the ridge of a massive barn, and the road swings left to give still further choice of route.

At a four-crossway one arm of the finger-post points straight ahead for Wooburn Common, and if that way is followed it leads between scrub and dense woodland to the

" Royal Standard ", whence by-roads and tracks radiate, and one particularly inviting field-path strikes across country towards Beaconsfield and the Green Line coach route back to Uxbridge and London. The left-hand of the four ways comes steeply up beside another high-banked wood from Wooburn " Town "—so called to distinguish the " church-town " from Wooburn Green, half a mile deeper in the hills. The right-hand way gives delightful going at any time of year, but especially on a bright winter day when the sunlight shines low between the bare trunks and brings light and colouring to the carpet of fallen leaves among the beech and the rich brown bracken among the thorn bushes. On either hand these open woodlands border the road, until it touches the fringe of Dropmore, where majestic beech and oak, well spaced-out by judicious felling of the fine timber, give space for great clumps of rhododendron. Some say that rhododendrons will not flourish on the chalk of the hills, but here at Dropmore they have found soil that

SPADE OAK REACH, ABOVE BOURNE END.

PASTORAL COUNTRY AND PLEASURE-SAILING.

suits them well enough to bring one back in summer to see the blooms.

Bearing left from Dropmore gate and left again round the well-kept thatch at the corner of Littleworth hamlet, the road runs on through open woods and scrub to fork among the gorse and broom and bracken of Littleworth Common. Foot-tracks, too, lead to and fro between the " Jolly Woodman " and the New Inn away across the turf where the pond is bordered by as fine a show of bulrushes as one sees in many a mile.

Close by the New Inn, where half a dozen tall, spare Scots pines tower behind the cottages, a footpath strikes away along the field-side by a wood, making across country towards Egypt Hill; and Egypt is known to every visitor to Burnham Beeches. Before it gets there, however, it meets an old bridle-path winding up a broad, shallow dip, and keeping exactly the line of the old route from Burnham to Beaconsfield. The present road swings uphill north-

westward by Littleworth, but the old ways from the river
into the hills always followed the line of least resistance as
far as they could. They kept to the easy going of the
valley bottoms, and never, if they could avoid it, slanted up
across a slope, for neither horses nor men care for slithering
along a sideways track that spoils the foothold.

However, the road that now runs curving down among
the beechwoods makes a truly beautiful route in either
direction. It turns right from the Beaconsfield–Slough
main road, and very soon swings round a bend that brings
a dense array of beeches close at hand on the left. An
open, gently-dropping half-mile leads straight to another
dark mass of woodland, but the road splits against its apex,
and the left fork, that tries to keep straight (to find and
continue that old bridle-path mentioned before) soon loses
itself among the Beeches with a capital " B ", for London's
own Burnham Beeches spread away up here to merge into
the country of this plateau. The other fork skirts beech-

THE TOW-PATH BETWEEN BOURNE END AND COOKHAM.

THE VILLAGE AND
CHURCH OF BRAY.

THE RIVERSIDE
NEAR BRAY,
BELOW
MAIDENHEAD.

wood for a mile and more before it finds Littleworth
Common spreading right and left; and only a half-mile
beyond, it also finds " Burnham Beeches " in the shape of
the inn at a road junction where another way from Dropmore comes in on the right.

Just beyond this inn, the road begins to drop more
sharply, and through the high hedge on the right a " Public
Footpath " sign points Thamesward.

It really does lead at once into unmistakable river-country.
One has only to climb over, or through, or under, the high
stile that bars the gap to survey rough meadow falling away
towards the flatter, richer pastures, fringed with elm and
oak, that stretch away southward to tall ranks of poplars
showing so surely that the Thames is not far away.

This road and this footpath are only single instances
of the many ways that are to be found threading the ups and
downs of this rural stretch of country. Four roads,
roughly parallel, give choice of north or southward routes,
besides the one that forms a majestic avenue between Dropmore and Cliveden, north-westerly from Burnham Gores.

That last name is itself a reminder of ancient customs.
Every dressmaker knows that a " gore " is a long, narrow
triangle fitted in between other pieces. So is a gore in
farming—a long, narrow triangle among odd-shaped fields,
or the slanting strip left at the side of a field when all the
square part has been ploughed. When the plough could
no longer cut straight up and back, and there was no head-
land for the team to turn, the " gore " that remained was left
to be planted with some other crop suitable for small casual
bits of ground. Here at the crossroad west of Burnham
village the gore attains substantial size, fifty yards wide at
the foot and stretching by the roadside for half a mile before
hedge and road converge.

Another strip can be found, eastward along Gore road

K

that runs from this road-junction towards " The Crispin " in Burnham village.

These north and south by-ways can provide abundance of variety on out and home journeys. Some of the inter-mediate tracks between them and the few inter-connecting links are worth exploring too—notably the almost over-grown bridle-way that emerges near the south-eastern corner of Dropmore. Thence a delightful by-lane skirts the lower side of the estate—another fine ramble, this, for a wintry day when the woods break the wind from the north and the sun shines low into them across the flat meadows between here and the river country. The road winds pleasantly past the ends of other farm tracks each of which find its own way down an age-old hollow; and when the next main road northward is reached, it is found to be none other than that stately avenue that bends left round the wall of Cliveden—a delightful route for yet another tour up-river. It runs gently downhill beside a high-banked wood, until suddenly the trees on both sides thin out to show a steep drop ahead, and the great sweeping curves of the Thames appear across the wide valley floor.

This is one of several points that give a pleasing sense of having discovered the " Upper Thames ", even though there is always a fresh aspect of the changeful, unchanging old river still further up, that merits the name still more.

For this hill-side, whence it is possible to see clearly the great S-shaped looping that the backwater makes from below Cookham Bridge to curl close under the foot of this bluff, is the point where yet another route returns to the Thames at Hedsor; and here is an instance of the irresistible way the Thames has of drawing the wanderer back for another look at its familiar corners and for fresh exploring of what is still to be seen.

## CHAPTER TEN

## RURAL BY-WAYS

THE bend of the river southward from Bourne End is one of the points that mark a change in the character of the Thames. It marks the river's farewell to the hills that have been bordering its northern bank all the way from Goring. It seems to be the end, too, of the meadows and farmlands that have, thus far, kept showing what a country river the Thames is, for private estates and gardens begin to close in on both sides of the narrowing valley.

Before following the river downwards, however, to see whether this is true or not, one can find still further interest round this meeting place of hills and valleys, large and small. The main valley here is almost at its widest: from Penn church-tower, the summit of Hindhead can occasionally be seen, thirty-six miles due south. Yet within that expanse, Hedsor Hill and Winter Hill face each other across the river's bend, only a mile apart. The minor undulations can provide especially good exploring ground just here, particularly along the edge of the hills that the Thames is forsaking.

The little side-valley of the Wye—one of the very minor tributaries—comes curling round the peninsula of Flackwell Heath, which has been noticed before as commanding magnificent views up and down the main valley. It forms a tongue of high land, rich in footpaths and by-ways among isolated hamlets which belong both to the river and to the hill country. From the brow of Hedsor Hill, a footpath branches half-right, to skirt the top of a steeply sloping field below the wood-edge, towards the tiny church of St. Nicholas crowning a rounded point of hill. Here, for many years, there burned a beacon that served to light land and water traffic through the maze of paths and streams across the levels below.

From here it is possible to look across and trace, on the map and on the ground, the paths along the hill-foot, well back from the low-lying northern bank. One path, already noted as leading from Well End towards Hedsor, was observed to have a branch heading away towards Wooburn, and keeping just far enough up the slope to ensure firm going when the levels were flooded. That branching path itself throws off several side-shoots, to Core's End, to Wooburn " Town ", and to Wooburn church, wherever a possible crossing of the Wye could be found; but it also holds on along the hill-side, to climb steeply up Juniper Hill to the " Green Dragon ", where it joins another track that has climbed up the very end of this ridge from Bourne End, winding pleasantly by field-sides and between woodlands and through rough scrub and brambles.

From the " Green Dragon ", a variety of by-ways can lead along the backbone of this little ridge, notably along the roadway known to Flackwell Heath as the Straight Bit— possibly because, as Mark Twain observed of the Street called Straight in Damascus, it is straighter than a corkscrew, but not as straight as a rainbow. In that direction, how- ever, one is led on and on into the Chiltern Hills, and paths into the valley below wait to lead the wanderer back to the Thames.

From the prominent landmark of a water-tower, close by Vicarage Farm, a track can be found dropping squarely down the hill-side north-eastward.

Looking level across the valley to the woodlands round

Penn, one can pick out pathways to Forty Green, to Knotty Green, and ultimately on towards Chalfont and the Misbourne Valley, which also curves in its turn down to the Thames.

Looking lower down one sees the great main Oxford road swooping down from Holtspur. Lower still, the eye cannot avoid the group of paper-mills that occupy a major part of this valley; but even among these there is interest.

The most prominent mill is easily identified with the name of " Glory Mill " on the map. Glory Hill winds up past it towards Holtspur, and Glory Hill Farm can be seen on the hill-brow; and the name goes back to times long before the days of paper-mills.

Long ago, there was a bishop's palace at Wooburn. The bishop was the one whose diocesan seat was noted in Chapter Two as being at Dorchester, in south Oxfordshire, before it was transferred to Lincoln. The visits of the bishop of that vast diocese to his Wooburn palace would naturally be so infrequent as to be something of an event. At the point where Glory Hill descends from the highway at Holtspur to join the valley road to Wooburn, there was placed a shrine. The bishop would be met there by his devoted people, chanting the " Gloria in Excelsis ". The shrine became known as the Bishop's Glory, and though the palace has been incorporated in Wooburn House, the name persists.

Half-way along towards Wooburn " Town " the valley road is joined by another Holtspur road at Wooburn Green. The green itself forms a tree-bordered triangle between the roads, and a variety of inns and shops and cottages line the three sides without much of note among them, except the public-house sign " The Queen and Albert ", which puts Queen Victoria and her consort firmly

THE WOODS OF
CLIVEDEN.

THE TARRY STONE
AT COOKHAM.

VIEW FROM WINTER
HILL, ABOVE
COOKHAM DEAN.

in the right order of precedence. The road that has descended hither from Holtspur, steep and high-banked below scrub and woodland, crosses the Wye stream just behind the village, and between the stream and the hill-foot, a riverside path from Glory Mill joins it, and continues, beyond the road, to climb the hill-side.

The expanse of scrub along the top of the slope here is threaded by several branches of this path, heading away over the breezy upland towards Beaconsfield. Still more paths climb the same hill-side behind Wooburn Town—a pleasant collection of dwellings round the church, which include the noble " Boscobel Barn ", with its magnificent beams and curious ancient carvings. The two quiet little streets that converge behind the church seem to lead nowhere else; but round a sharp bend at the very apex, a lane that curves below a steep bank crowned with beechwood is found striking up the steep face of Wash Hill.

A path from the corner strikes left to the remote hill-top hamlet of Berghers Hill; and to the right a path diverges southward, to cross Kiln Lane above Core's End and bring the wayfarer back to Harvest Hill, to look down once more on Heaven's Lea, and Hedsor Wharf, and Cock Marsh stretching level beyond the curve of the river.

Any journey that can be planned through this rural back-water will be worth remembering—especially if the route includes a descent of Hedsor Hill.

This hill, be it noted, is very sharp and steep, with a perilous bend and cross-way at the foot. A cautious descent, with halts here and there, has thus the double merit of safety and of enabling one to glance around in as many directions as possible—left to the woods from Winter Hill towards Cookham Dean, ahead to an especially clear and green rise of sky-line above Sheepridge, and to the right for the many-coloured woodlands of Hedsor Park.

AN EXAMPLE OF THAMES VALLEY SCENERY FROM THE HILLS ABOVE STREATLEY.

The cross-way at the foot of the hill is typical, in combining roads and footpaths, of the by-ways of this country. To the right is a private drive, but it is also the start of an inalienable public footpath—a church-path up the hill-side field that is crowned by the little bell-turret of St. Nicholas. The fingerpost also indicates " Footpath to Wooburn Common and Beaconsfield "; for here begins one more of those ways that traverse the hills which here reach down so close to the river. In this rural quadrangle of upland bounded by Bath road, Oxford road, and river, travellers of all kinds can ramble comparatively near home. Motorists and cyclists can thread its by-ways on a variety of round trips that seldom extend more than twenty-five miles from London. Pathfinders can choose a variety of starting and return points on the bus routes through Slough or through Beaconsfield, or on the road connecting those towns, or, on the fourth side, on the High Wycombe–Maidenhead–Windsor route of the Thames Valley bus service, which follows the Wye to Bourne End, and thence keeps fairly close to the main river.

This cross-way at the foot of Hedsor Hill is within easy reach of that last-named return route, though as one stands there it seems almost buried in the hills. The fourth arm of the signpost also gives a double direction : " Private Road to Hedsor Wharf; Public Footpath to Cookham ".

This way dips down between wooded banks to the " private " entrance. To the right, however, a swing-gate stands invitingly as swing-gates always do, and very soon a planked bridge spans another minor confluent of the Thames that winds gently beneath a line of pollard willows. Across the field beyond, a clear path leads straight ahead; but it is the edge of the field to the left that invites the walker, for here flows the Thames itself, wide, deep, and strong-running between more willows on the near side and the river's own poplars beyond. Coots flutter across or swim jerkily to their hiding-holes, for this is a stretch of river quite undisturbed by the traffic that throngs through Cookham Lock. The way through the lock has a picture-book view down-stream towards the woods of Cliveden, but this side-stream (one hardly likes to call it a backwater, for it has all the character of the authentic River Thames) has the extra charm of showing the river at its rural best, as it swings its great curve through these meadows, from the weir to the foot of the wooded bluff.

The path leads ahead towards a thin line of silver birches, with darker woods behind screening Cookham church tower, to strike the road a few yards short of Cookham

Bridge. Across the bridge, the road curves past the church into the foot of Cookham village.

Here, three roads meet; four, in fact, if one counts the " No Through Road " to the left, which leads riverwards again to a bridge arching over still another arm of the river. Across it, Odney Common stretches into the distance, bounded by more lines of poplars and by the converging branches of the Thames which make this both an island in the river and an island of quiet roaming-space below the high bank of woods up the hill-side.

That road-junction at Cookham is no ordinary village street-corner and bus stop. It appears in the time-table as " Cookham, Tarry Stone "; and by the wall north-east, the Tarry Stone stands. This massive boulder formerly stood in the middle of the cross-way, serving for years as a mounting block, and also marking the spot where, as a bronze plate tells, " Sports were held before 1587 ". Tradition says it was a meteorite, though geological theories differ; it has been a landmark and cherished possession of Cookham for centuries.

Fine old brick houses, with jasmine and wistaria climbing to their cornices and tiled roofs, make this a pleasant corner for observation. Westward, too, the village street shows a varied assortment of timbered cottages among Cookham's well-known hotels—" Bel and the Dragon " on the right, and the " King's Arms " opposite. The street leads in a few hundred yards to the open expanse of Cookham Moor, with a footway crossing it by a raised causeway.

As an alternative to the Boulter's Lock road from the Tarry Stone, another way to Maidenhead turns left by " The Gate " public-house beyond the Moor, and runs through open country, without any great scenic attraction but pleasantly rural, on the western side of the railway. Farther west still the ground slopes upward towards the

A TYPICAL THAMES-COUNTRY BY-ROAD, FROM THE SLOPE OF THE BERKSHIRE
DOWNS.

ridge that culminates in Quarry Woods overlooking Marlow; and any who still seek woodland wanderings may fare onwards past " The Gate " and over the railway by Cookham station. A local bus can ease the climb by Cookham Rise to " The Chequers " at Cookham Dean, and there one finds paths and by-ways radiating in every direction.

One quick way to the hill-top is a path to the right at the telephone-box a few yards above " The Chequers "; this climbs steeply between gardens and orchards to the open crest of Winter Hill, where Spade Oak Reach suddenly appears below. Another lane that steepens sharply beyond this footpath-turn, curves suddenly round a sloping expanse of green, with the war memorial cross at the top, and the sign of the " Hare and Hounds " pointing to a delightful group of dwellings on the verge of another deep dell.

Opposite the " Chequers ", still more lanes can be seen circling and diverging up the slope. Among them Pope's Lane may be selected as one of the many routes to this little ridge-top, where paths plunge down towards Marlow through Quarry Woods. A pleasant, level road between the upper edge of the woods and the fields that sink away towards Maidenhead can be followed past the " Uncle Tom's Cabin " towards Pinkneys Green, where the Marlow–Maidenhead road winds up along the other side of the woodland; or a turn left, signposted " Cookham ", bears downhill with open farmland dropping away on the right.

From here, a footpath strikes across the fields, past a spinney where rooks build in the elms, and the two spires of Maidenhead show prominently ahead for those who choose this homeward route—rural almost to the end— from yet another patch of country well worth exploring. Is there any limit to the possibilities of such Thames-country wanderings? Keep on exploring, and see.

# INDEX

# ACKNOWLEDGMENTS

The publishers have pleasure in acknowledging their obligation to the photographers whose work illustrates the following pages:—

The Mustograph Agency: xii, 8, 11, 14, 16, 19, 29, 66, 83, 89, 91, 95, 100, 102, 103, 106, 110, 114, 120, 127, 140, 143.

Mr. E. W. Tattersall: *Frontispiece*, 13, 132, 138, and *Jacket*.

Fox Photos, Ltd.: 2, 26, 29, 31, 39, 42, 44, 54, 61, 68, 75, 105, 118, 120, 129, 130, 131.

Mr. Staniland Pugh: 3, 21, 22, 32, 34, 37, 53, 62, 64, 68, 75, 138.

Sport and General: 112, 116, 128.

Messrs. Dorien Leigh, Ltd.: 5, 13, 122.

Mr. F. A. Girling: 6, 7.

Humphrey and Vera Joel: 15, 56, 122.

Mr. George Long: 17, 47, 48, 52, 73, 79, 89, 90, 96, 98, 105, 138.

Mr. H. J. Smith: 29, 34, 71, 79, 85, 86, 100.

Great Western Railway: 54, 95.

Mr. F. W. Simms, 4.